Family
for
Life

How to have happy,
healthy relationships
with your adult children

KATHY PEEL

McGraw-Hill

New York   Chicago   San Francisco   Lisbon   London
Madrid   Mexico City   Milan   New Delhi   San Juan
Seoul   Singapore   Sydney   Toronto

The *McGraw·Hill* Companies

1 2 3 4 5 6 7 8 9 0   DOC/DOC   0 9 8 7 6 5 4 3

ISBN 0-07-140725-1

McGraw-Hill books are available at special discounts to use as premiums and sales promotions, or for use in corporate training programs. For more information, please write to the Director of Special Sales, Professional Publishing, McGraw-Hill, Two Penn Plaza, New York, NY 10121-2298. Or contact your local bookstore.

Library of Congress Cataloging-in-Publication Data

Peel, Kathy, 1951-
   Family for life : how to have happy, healthy relationships with your adult children / by Kathy Peel.
      p. cm.
Includes index.
   ISBN 0-07-140725-1 (pbk. : alk. paper)
   1. Parenting. 2. Parent and child. 3. Family. I. Title.
HQ755.8.P43 2003
649'.1—dc21
                                    2002156358

In Memory of

Judith Louise Musgrave

Friend, role model, mentor. Judy taught me through
the way she lived her life what it means to be a loving wife,
good mother, and fun grandmother.

Acknowledgments

Although the author's name appears on the cover, every book is a group effort. I am blessed to have a wonderful team of people who have contributed to this book.

Special thanks to Nancy Hancock, Executive Editor at McGraw Hill, for allowing me to write this book. Thanks also to Meg Leder for her able editorial assistance and helpful attitude.

A special tribute to my good friend and colleague Patti Dematteo, CEO of Ultimate Performance, who believes in my mission to strengthen families and help make home a warm and welcoming place for family and friends.

For their expert editing and going the extra mile, sincere appreciation goes to Ann Matturro Gault, Holly Halverson, and Maureen Connolly. And for their research assistance, a big thanks to Jill Dalley, Martha Hook, and Debbie Zadina.

Thank you to the many mothers, fathers, adult children, and family therapists who took part in interviews and anonymously shared their stories and advice.

And to my incredibly supportive family—my husband Bill, and our three sons, John, Joel, and James—I am thankful can write this book with confidence because of what we've experienced and learned the past thirty-one years. I love you all.

Contents

Introduction

Parenting, like war, is a lot easier to begin than it is to end.

—David Jeremiah

*I*n the film *Parenthood* the sixty-four-year-old grand-father (Jason Robards) describes to his thirty-five-year-old son (Steve Martin) the anguish he felt as the parent of a young child:

> We thought you had polio; for a week we didn't know. I hated going through all that caring, and worry, and pain. And it's not like that all ends when your kid's eighteen, or twenty-one, or sixty-one. It never, never ends. In parenting there is no end zone. You never cross the goal line, spike the ball, and do your touchdown dance. *Never.*

When my husband, Bill, and I became parents for the first time almost twenty-nine years ago, we naively thought that after a few years of potty training, Band-Aids, driver's ed, first dates, and SAT prep courses, the hard part would be over. We'd launch our children—with their framed diplomas, strong values, and positive self-images—into the real world and go home, empty nesters eager to reap the rewards of those count-less Saturday mornings spent at the soccer field.

But to the surprise of many ready-to-cruise moms and dads, parenting doesn't stop when you think it will. Kids drop out of college in search of what really matters (parents pay for the expedition). College graduates suspect that corporate culture could be stifling ("I could never be a nine-to-five person") and opt to save money by living at home while awaiting the perfect job. Wedding galas that cost a small fortune sometimes end in divorce, sending hurting children back to the nest—this time with their own brood.

So our job continues, but in many ways parenting older children isn't so different from parenting younger ones. After all, there are bullies in the business world just as there were on the playground. And we're still training our children, making them feel better, and helping them through life's inevitable tests. Only this time, the wounds don't heal with a Band-Aid and choosing the wrong answer can have far-reaching consequences.

---

*Making the decision to have a child is momentous—
it is to decide forever to have your heart go walking
around outside your body.*

—Elizabeth Stone

Today, as the mother of older children (ages twenty-eight, twenty-five, and eighteen), I find that my parenting style has changed. Now, instead of issuing motherly mandates ("Please finish your broccoli"; "Clean up your room"), I offer low-key counsel ("Do you think you should wear a tie to that interview?" "It probably would be a good idea to get another estimate"). When they need me, I strive to step in without stepping over the line and offer support without being suffocating. While sometimes instinct guides me well—one son recently thanked me for warning him about a bogus deal that seemed too good to be true—I've learned some lessons the hard way, and I'd like to help you avoid some of my mistakes.

The goal of this book is to guide you in your "new" roles as parent of a grown child, in-law, and grandparent. You'll find positive and practical ways to help an older child be a successful adult gleaned not only from my three decades of child-raising experience but from the input of countless parents of older children, the "kids" themselves, and marriage and family experts. The families I interviewed represent a very wide age span and varied locations and situations, yet all of what I heard kept boiling down to eight strategies:

- Build a bridge between generations

- Prepare kids well for the big world

- Mend broken fences and love in ways that matter

- Be a dreambuilder (not a dreambuster)

- Keep the porch light on and the home fire burning

- Keep your clan connected

- Be a *great* grandparent

- Don't neglect to nurture yourself

Each chapter will offer some ideas as well as some dos and don'ts. Not all of them will be right for your family. As you read through them, choose a few to try that feel right for where you are in your parenting pilgrimage, that seem in harmony with the personalities and circumstances of your children.

You'll find in these pages many quotes from sages both new and old. Almost thirty years ago I began a collection of clever words from a wide variety of sources: ancient philosophers, Dear Abby, the Bible, great leaders, people I admire. Why? Because I feel that I need all the help and wise counsel I can get. I want passionately to continue to learn how to navigate the joyous, mysterious, challenging, sometimes dicey waters of parenting. The way I see it, there's so much to learn and keep learning, why not learn from someone else's experience? Maybe I can avoid a few hard knocks. Why not, with the help of those who have been there, done that or those who are astute about life and relationships, make my parenting path a little smoother?

> *Learn from others what to pursue and what to avoid,*
> *and let your teachers be the lives of others.*
> —Dionysius Cato

Wisdom always works, whatever its source, and I think you'll discover, as I did, that the time-tested counsel of ancient as well as more modern sages functions consistently and surprisingly well. Although these folks probably didn't imagine that their writings would be used as parenting advice, smart ideas always bring smart results when they are applied intelligently. I hope these quotes are as useful for you as they have been for me.

> *The best educated human is the one who understands*
> *most about the life in which he is placed.*
> —Helen Keller

I don't pretend to have a perfect family, but I can say with all honesty that we're a one-for-all, all-for-one team. I mean, we must have done something right—all three of our grown sons actually still want to spend time with us. In fact, during the summer, as we were driving home from a wonderful day of Fourth of July activities, our youngest son commented, unprompted: "I know that even when my brothers and I have families of our own, we'll want to keep having fun together. I love being part of such a close family."

Talk about hitting the parenting jackpot! As a mother starring in *The Peel Family Story,* Act II, I felt as rich as a billionaire when I heard that sentiment. As we grow older and our family expands, each of us is committed to enjoying the blessings of life together, supporting each other through the tough times, and helping each other develop to his or her individual potential. Parenting is a great privilege and an ongoing responsibility, and there is no greater role in life.

Family life is the source of the greatest human happiness.
—Robert J. Gavighurst

So as you take yourself out of center field and find a seat on the parenting sidelines, have faith in the lives you've nurtured. Although you're no longer calling the shots, your kids still need cheerleaders, and parents are their biggest fans. Don't feel surprised if you feel a little displaced when they leave the nest; that's perfectly normal. The good news is that if we handle the preparing and letting-go processes well, usually by the time the curtain goes up in *Parenting,* Act II, we've been cast in our new role: that of trusted adviser and friend. If you feel a bit overwhelmed, take heart: Every day is a new day, and it's never too late to make changes, mend fences, discover new ways of loving your kids, and work on the most important thing in the world—your family.

1

Build a Bridge Between Generations

The family. We were a strange little band of charac-ters trudging through life sharing diseases and tooth-paste, coveting one another's desserts, hiding shampoo, borrowing money, locking each other out of our rooms, inflicting pain and kissing to heal it in the same instant, loving, laughing, defending, and trying to figure out the common thread that bound us all together.

—Erma Bombeck

*I*t used to drive me nuts when my folks talked about the dif-ficulties of growing up during the Depression. Compared with what they "went through," my problems as a carefree teenager in the 1960s seemed silly. Of course they complained about the music and how the Beatles needed a haircut, how I didn't appreciate indoor plumbing and the value of a dime—that kind of stuff. But honestly, did all parents really have to walk five miles to school in knee-deep snow back then?

Now my husband and I catch ourselves doing the same thing to our kids. We complain about music and hair, how they don't appreciate modern technology and the value of a dollar. They have no idea what it was like to type a paper back in the "old days" on a manual typewriter rather than a computer screen with spell check. As tempting as it is, this kind of communication is as helpful to our kids as it was to us—not very. And it sends the same message: Mom and Dad are hopelessly out of touch.

I'm starting to wonder what my folks were up to at my age that makes them so doggoned suspicious of me all the time.

—Margaret Blair

Drawing comparisons can be enlightening if you can help your kids see how one generation shapes the next. My fellow baby boomers and I lived in a very different world. We used telephones mounted on the wall that didn't come with answering machines. Our hair dryers had plastic caps. We used slide rules in math class and listened to music from 45- or 33-rpm records. When we talked about the draft, we weren't talking about sports, and somehow we managed to stay entertained with just three channels on TV. My kids are typical of today's high-tech young adults. They're so tuned in, they can't imagine life without cable, computers, and cell phones.

Young men think old men are fools; but old men know young men are fools.

—George Chapman

Other huge differences: During the 1950s and 1960s young people typically graduated from high school, attended college, joined the armed forces, or found full-time work and became self-supporting. Many married in their late teens or early twenties, had kids right away, and bought their first houses. Extended families often lived close together, and so even after marriage the kids gathered regularly at the family home, usually for Sunday dinner. Grandparents enjoyed occasional baby-sitting and anticipated an easy retirement.

This was the norm. Today, when kids finally do get out on their own—which for many happens in their midtwenties—they typically live more than a hundred miles away and often in another state. Marriage takes place much later now, at the average age of thirty rather than twenty. And today grandparents often find themselves in a little deeper than occasional baby-sitting. According to the U.S. census for the year 2000, 2.3 million American grandparents are responsible for raising one or more of their grandchildren—not the golden years they probably had in mind.

Divorce is another factor. Forty percent of young adults come from broken homes, and countless others grew up practically without parents: Mom and Dad both worked, so no one was home for them after school. Sadly, many associate *family* not with "happily ever after" but with loneliness and pain. One young woman who was forced to fend for herself while her mother and father feuded echoed a comment I've heard from many people her age: "I don't know if I'll ever marry or have children," she shared. "I don't think I can handle more heartache."

Don't limit a child to your own learning, for he was born in another time.

—Rabbinical saying

Attitude about work is another generational difference. Today's adult children aren't as married to their work. They change jobs often and work fewer hours than their parents did.

A banker recently told me that he could count on an employee thirty years old or younger staying less than four months on the job. A friend in the publishing business commented that her assistant works hard all day, but when the clock strikes five, she's out of there—no matter how much work is left undone. I've heard the same lament from countless other employers: New recruits attach no sentiment to the company they work for, and they want the rewards of a job well done now, if not sooner. They seem to have more time for travel, hobbies, and sports. They long for the freedom to live the life *they* want— the life many believe they deserve.

Unfortunately, many of today's young adults are starting off life on their own with a lot of debt. "Don't wait, buy now. Easy credit available." "Bad credit? No problem!" They've heard this Madison Avenue mantra over and over, day after day. We have become a population that wants what it wants when it wants it. We're like the screaming two-year-old I saw in the grocery store this week who wanted candy, and he wanted it *now*! Our kids have grown up in a culture in which delayed gratification is an anomaly. "Buy now, pay later" is the norm; thus, our children have not experienced the satisfaction of working and saving money to buy something they've always dreamed of with cash.

THE COSTLY PAYOFF

But parents and kids alike are now paying for this upbringing, because a big stepping-stone on the path to becoming a mature adult is learning to delay gratification. This means putting off something we want to do, such as buying a new giant-screen TV or going to the beach, to do something we have to do, such as saving our money or painting the house. Many young adults simply don't get this, an attitude that makes parents throw up their hands in exasperation. "What are they thinking?" we ask.

That's actually a very good question for parents to ponder. What *are* they thinking, and where did they learn to think like that? To be sure, the media have hyped instant gratification, but what about us? Could it be that we (their parents) have modeled a lifestyle of acquiring, or could it be that we've tried to show love to our children by buying them things?

Many of today's young adults grew up at a time when it was easier for parents to buy a child a new toy than to take him or her fishing. In many families, since both Mom and Dad had careers outside the home, they had more money than time, and so giving their kids things was easier than hanging out with them. The children sure liked getting new gadgets, and so it all seemed to work.

But unconsciously we were creating an addiction in our children that was based on the law of diminishing returns—the more we get, the more we need to satisfy us—which in the case of parenting goes something like this: You buy a three-year-old an inexpensive toy. The toy pleases and occupies the child for a short while, but then he becomes bored and wants a new toy. This time you buy him a slightly bigger and more costly toy, which may please him for a little while longer, but soon it too becomes old and dull. The child continues to want more and more, and you continue to buy more and more.

Parents in any income bracket can fall into this trap. Practice this pattern for twenty years, and, well, as our parents' generation used to say, "The proof's in the pudding."

I bring this up not to say that we're sorry parents who should forever berate ourselves for creating this monstrous cycle. Guilt trips are seldom, if ever, a productive part of problem solving, but knowing the facts you've got to work with is. The attitudes and behaviors of the younger generation can be maddening. It's tempting to confront their unrealistic expectations with cynicism: "Wake up to reality! Life is no fairy tale. No one owes you anything. Get real!" But angry comments only widen the gap. Peace begins with a willingness to understand things from another point of view.

If it was going to be easy to raise kids, it never would have started with something called labor.

—Author unknown

The lesson here for all is to get behind the attitudes, and by doing so you probably will discover common ground, sometimes in surprising areas. A recent study of twenty- to thirty-year-olds revealed that 87 percent plan to marry just once, and 64 percent consider their personal lives more important than their professional lives. Doesn't that sound like something that parents would list as a desire for their children? Maybe we're more on the same page than we realized.

BEEN THERE

I have children, grandchildren, and great-grandchildren, and I can tell you that about every ten years styles change and issues shift in our culture. But the principles of being a good parent never change. It's the same today as it was sixty-five years ago when I was raising my children. You've got to teach kids what's right and what's wrong and show them that in how you live your own life. And you've got to love kids unconditionally, whether they're twenty or fifty. That doesn't mean you agree with them on every issue or approve of all of their behavior or choices. It does mean that you love them and you tell them so. Every human being, no matter how rebellious or how he's failed, has something lovable about him. Look for that something.

—Myra, Age 83

It seems clear that today's young adults want to avoid the mistakes many of us baby-boomer parents made: workaholism and divorce among them. Isn't that wise? Think of it: Our children may be the ones to break the disturbing cycles of family failure. They aspire to a satisfying and healthy family life as well as a career. They're aiming high, and they just may hit their target!

Be nice to your children, for they will choose your rest home.
                                                            —Phyllis Diller

---

Therefore, the next time a generation gap discussion starts to get out of hand, take a deep breath and remind your kids that you're the same age as Mick Jagger.

BUILDING A BRIDGE: THE NECESSARY TOOLS

Following are some key components to maintaining a high-quality relationship with your older kids and building bridges for communication.

1. Patience

Be patient, and remember you were once in their shoes. Many parents of young adults say they're frustrated because their kids won't listen to them: The kids think they know it all. But think about it: Didn't you know it all when you were in your twenties?

I am not young enough to know everything.
                                    —Oscar Wilde

Almost 3,000 years ago King Solomon wrote these words: "What has been will be again, what has been done will be done again; there is nothing new under the sun." If we take that ancient bit of wisdom to heart, we shouldn't be surprised that we shake our heads in dismay at our kids, just as our parents shook their heads in dismay at us, just as their parents shook their heads in dismay at them. The generation gap is not a new idea.

When I was a boy of fourteen, my father was so ignorant I could hardly stand to have the old man around. But when I got to be twenty-one, I was astonished at how much he had learned in seven years.
                                    —Mark Twain

If your young adult is in the stage where she's always ready to give to those older than she the full benefit of her experience, hang in there. Just as it happened in your life, and your parents' lives, and your grandparents' lives, there will come a day when your child will wake up—usually after a difficult or painful experience—and realize that she may not be as smart as she thought she was and that she still has at least a few things to learn. Life has a way of quenching the arrogance of youth.

2. Trust

Create a safe environment for communication. Here's an important question: When your son or daughter comes face to face with reality and is searching for the way to live successfully and make good decisions, will he or she want to talk to you? Are you considered a safe, supportive, and reliable source of counsel or a source of criticism?

Have a heart that never hardens, and a temper that never fires, and a touch that never hurts.
—Charles Dickens

My husband and I consider it a great honor that our adult children ask our opinion and confide in us frequently. Believe me, we didn't figure out on our own how to have this kind of rewarding relationship. Over the years we watched parents ahead of us in the game who had the kind of relationship with their older children that we wanted to have with ours. We asked those parents to share what had worked and not worked in their families and what advice they'd give to us as our children were growing from adolescence to adulthood. Years ago our son's sixty-year-old kindergarten teacher summed her parenting advice up like this: *Love covers a multitude of sins.* If our kids can trust our love—no matter what—that fact will override a lot of parenting mistakes we make.

From birth to death, every person wants to know, "Am I loved unconditionally?" If any person feels that he or she constantly has to try out to be on our team, we will drive that person away. In a world where performance means everything, our kids need to know the tryouts are over. They've already made our team, and nothing they do will cause us to put them on waivers.

When we consistently give our children the message that our love for them is conditional and is based on their behavior, we exasperate them. Messages such as "I love you if you make the dean's list," "I love you if you come home for Thanksgiving," and "I love you if you weigh 115 pounds" are messages we can't afford to send if we want a high-quality relationship with our older children.

3. Restraint

Here's some other good advice we received: *Listen more than you talk, and when you do talk, be careful what you say.*

Don't feel you have to *advise* older teens and young adults as much as *listen* to them. It's easy to be so eager to help them that we voice opinions and give advice before we hear them out. Many parents discover in retrospect that what would have been most helpful was just a loving, nonjudgmental attitude and a shoulder to lean on when needed.

In case of doubt, it is always better to say too little than too much.
—Thomas Jefferson

My husband and I have been married one year. Something I've come to appreciate about my parents is that they provide a "safe" environment for us to talk about issues and ask advice. They listen a lot and don't criticize us. His parents don't do that at all, so we don't share things with them.

—Sally, age 25

The words we use to get a point across to an older child are extremely important. For example:

Don't say: "When I was your age, I . . ."
Instead say: "I know we see things differently. Tell me how
            you see the situation."

Don't say: "I'm older and wiser than you."
Instead say: "I disagree with you about that, but tell me your
            point of view."

Don't say: "You shouldn't feel like that."
Instead say: "How you feel is important to me. Tell me why
            you feel that way."

Don't say: "I told you so!"
Instead say: "We all make mistakes. The important thing is
            that we learn from them."

Don't say: "How could you do this to me?"
Instead say: "Each of us is responsible for his or her actions—
            how they affect others as well as ourselves."

29 THINGS YOU SHOULD NEVER SAY TO A CHILD OF ANY AGE

1. You're just no good.

2. You'll never amount to anything.

3. You got what you deserved.

4. What's wrong with you?

5. When are you going to act your age?

6. Can't you do anything right?

7. I've had it with you.

8. All you ever do is cause trouble.

9. Just wait until you have kids.

10. When will you ever learn?

11. You are stupid.

12. You are lazy.

13. Who do you think you are?

14. You'll be the death of me yet.

15. Haven't I taught you anything?

16. You need to have your head examined.

17. Don't you care about anything?

18. What makes you think you're so special?

19. Don't you ever listen?

20. When are you going to start listening to me?

21. If I've told you once, I've told you a million times.

22. I can't wait until you're gone.

23. Why can't you be more like your sister (brother)?

24. You are so much trouble.

25. I don't know why I had kids.

26. How could you do this to me?

27. You're just like your father (mother)!

28. When I was your age, I . . .

29. Because I said so, that's why.

4. Understanding

Try to understand their world. Stay with me here; this is important. Think of some of the people in your life with whom you have a good rapport. Maybe they're people you met during a political campaign or at an exercise class or book club. Maybe they're neighbors or coworkers or people you met at church. Whoever they are, you have a meaningful relationship because you've shared parts of each other's worlds. More than likely you don't agree on everything, but you appreciate and accept each other's frame of reference.

It's not too big of a leap to see that the same principles apply in a relationship with our kids. What do we know about their worlds? What are their favorite television programs? What books are they reading? What films have influenced their lives? What's "in" and "out" fashionwise? What are their opinions about the state of the world? What music do they listen to, and what do the lyrics mean?

Our greatest obligation to our children is to prepare them to understand and to deal effectively with the world in which they will live and not with the world we have known or the world we would prefer to have.
—Grayson Kirk

Purposefully looking for ways to promote understanding and appreciation between generations is the first strategy for building rapport with an adult child. It's only natural to share your past (the good *and* the bad) with your kids. It helps them understand who you are, which is often the first step in understanding who they are. Personal anecdotes—delivered with the right amount of sensitivity—can be powerful medicine for a heartbroken or deeply disappointed son or daughter. Children need to know that the current difficult page in the story of their lives is not the final chapter.

For example, your daughter who scores lower than she anticipated on the SAT probably will feel better if she hears that the same thing happened to you. Knowing that you had to take the test three times before gaining acceptance to the college you wanted to attend gives her reason to believe she can do it too. Your son and daughter-in-law, worn out from staying up half the night with their colicky newborn, may take hope from hearing about the late nights when you and your husband took turns rocking him—and eventually the colic finally went away as the doctor predicted.

It's an old cliché, but it's still true in any relationship: People don't care how much you know until they know how much you care. Seeking to understand your young adult's world goes a long way toward paving the road of a good connection between the two of you.

5. Respect

Look for opportunities to show respect to your adult children. Choose not to generalize when you hear a reporter describe Gen-Xers as "the lazy generation." Of course, there are some in that age bracket who fall into that category. But don't forget that your own generation had its share of potheads, flower children, and unpatriotic flag burners. Look for good character attributes not just in the younger generation but in your own children, and tell them when you find them. Whether their behavior deserves respect may at times be in question, but young men and women always deserve our personal respect, our regard for them as valuable persons.

Respect their Opinions. One of the most important things we can do for our children is to let them think for themselves as adults—become independent thinkers. It's not our job to think for them but to train them and release them to form their own values. We've all known adults who can't think for themselves, who still depend on Mom or Dad for their opinions. When you find yourself in a disagreement with a son or daughter, be careful of the following phrases, which show disrespect for their opinions.

- That's ridiculous.
- You don't know what you are talking about.
- Only fools believe . . .
- It's a proven fact that . . .
- There's no question about . . .

Statements like these shut down conversation and relationship. They are negative emotional responses and defensiveness.

Try to find more agreeable ways to disagree and still show respect for your son or daughter's opinion. Here are some less offensive ways to express disagreement that affirm the value of the individual and keep the door open for more communication:

- I hear what you're saying, but it does raise a red flag for me.
- Can I share a different perspective with you?
- Correct me if I'm wrong, but I see a problem.
- I'm not sure I agree. Could I hear that again?
- Have you ever considered this perspective?

Respect Their Abilities. Several years ago I met a man in his midthirties who worked for his father in the family business. It looked like a pretty sweet deal until I saw them interact. The son could never please his dad. Even though the son was paid a six-figure salary, he couldn't do anything right, according to his father. After working for his father for ten years the son had never been allowed to make a decision on his own and, more important, to fail or succeed on his own.

Respect Their Decisions. It can be painful to watch our children make decisions that we know might hurt them, but they need to learn to fail and succeed on their own. How else will they ever learn? After giving them your counsel, step back and let them decide. They'll learn more by falling on their faces a few times than they can any other way, and we have to be willing to let them fail or they won't grow. When you find that they were right after all—which, by the way, will happen now and again—be sure to admit you were wrong and commend them. And of course, when you were right and they were wrong, grit your teeth and refuse to say, "If you'd only listened to your mother!"

Respect Their Privacy. You don't need to know every detail of their lives.

Respect Their Independence. Give them space.

6. Appreciation

What can you appreciate about what the younger generation has to offer? Their tech-savviness? Their healthy emphasis on having a life as well as a career? The importance they place on relationships? Tell them about the good you see.

I firmly believe kids don't want your understanding. They want your trust, your compassion, your blinding love and your car keys.

—Erma Bombeck

Encouraging words show that you value your son or daughter for who he or she is. Although we want to see improvement, we accept a person without demanding change. When we affirm people's value by our words or actions, we remind them that they are loved and esteemed.

ASKING QUESTIONS THAT COUNT

Deepen your relationship with your young adult by spending a little concentrated time with her, doing something you both enjoy. To break the ice, try the method used by one of the greatest teachers of all time. Socrates asked his students questions, hoping to open their minds by urging them to give a more profound consideration of the issues. His point was always to reveal how much more a student needed to learn.

Questions show that you are genuinely interested in your young adult and care about his thoughts and feelings. Questions let you find out just how much of your parental training is taking root; the child's answers will reveal much about where he is in moral development. Also, questions inspire your child to think through and establish his own values and standards for living.

It is better to ask some of the questions than to know all of the answers.

—James Thurber

Following are some questions to get the conversation rolling. As simple as it may sound, sometimes it's hard for parents to think of questions beyond "How was your day?" or "How's it going?" Nonspecifics like these typically don't encourage conversation or the sharing of information. Instead, try this: At natural times or places to carry on a conversation, such as when you're in the car on the way to a flea market in a neighboring town, walking from hole to hole on the golf course, or casting by the side of a stream, be prepared with some questions from this list.

Don't ask a lot of questions at once. You don't want your child to feel that she's on the witness stand. Just choose two or three for the first visit and then choose some new ones for the next time you get together. There's space at the end of the list for you to write some questions of your own.

- Describe what a really good friend is like. Do you have a friend like that? Are you a friend like that to anyone?

- When you walk into a room filled with people, what's the first thing that crosses your mind?

- Describe a time when you were really afraid.

- If you could eat dinner with three people, who would they be?

- What is the most difficult thing you've ever had to do?

- Would you rather watch *Survivor* or be on the show yourself?

- If you could ask God for three things, what would you request?

- Who is the bravest person you know?

- If you could travel back in time, what period of history would you like to experience firsthand?

- What are your three favorite songs?

- What are your three favorite desserts?

- If you could travel anyplace in the world, where would you go?

- What new hobby would you like to learn?

- What do you see yourself doing in ten years?
- What is your favorite restaurant?
- What are your three favorite movies of all time?
- What do you think it means to be in love?
- If you could relive one moment in your life, what would it be?
- What is your definition of success?
- Describe your dream career.
- What are the three things you worry about most?
- What are five things you want to do before you're forty?
- What do you think are the greatest things you've got going for you as you look toward the future?
- What would you do to make the world a better place?
- What characteristics do you want your future wife (husband) to have?
- What qualities will make you a good husband (wife)?
- What is your most embarrassing moment?
- What is the best book you've ever read?
- If someone gave you a million dollars, what would you do with it?
- What's the best gift you've ever received?
- What character traits do you admire in a person?
- _____
- _____
- _____

Once the conversation gets going, you may be surprised at how many personal qualities, dreams, and ideas your child shares with you, how alike you are on the inside. The generational chasm may actually shrink before your eyes! If this happens, you have begun to build some strong lines of communication with your older child that will serve you both all of your lives.

You never really understand a person until you consider things from his point of view—until you climb into his skin and walk around in it.

—Harper Lee,
To Kill a Mockingbird

GUIDELINES FOR PARENTING CHILDREN (OF ANY AGE)

When our boys were young, Bill and I realized we had a lot to learn about a very important job. It was perplexing to us that you have to get a license to cut hair, sell real estate, and participate in many other careers but no training is required for a person to become a parent. We put a high priority on learning to parent as best we could by immersing ourselves in books about child-raising, attending seminars, and learning from successful parents we knew. Everything we studied and read seemed to boil down to five attributes.

The following five guidelines helped pave the way for a close relationship with each of our boys. Interestingly, now that two of them are out on their own and one is on his way to college, we've realized that the same five objectives still apply, and continue to guide us as our role has shifted from parenting to closing the gap and becoming a mentor and friend, although now we express them in different ways. I encourage you, along with us, to make these your guidelines as well.

1. *Be fair.* We must let go of our kids and not make unreasonable demands on their time and attention. This includes being sensitive to their need to become independent.

2. *Be firm.* Just as it's wrong to expect our adult children to have their lives revolve around us, we don't let them expect us to have our lives revolve around them.

3. *Be fun.* Many entertaining things vie for our adult children's attention. We should ask ourselves: "Is coming home a fun thing? Do they want to get together with us, or do they dread being with us?"

4. *Be flexible.* It's as true now as it was when they were young: Adapting and rolling with the punches of parenthood is key to being a good parent. The only constant in life is change.

5. *Be affirming.* Every human being, no matter what her age, needs to be reminded of her value and unique contribution, how she is making a difference in the world.

It's Never Too Late

A forty-five-year-old friend told me how for the first time he is enjoying a warm relationship with his parents. "I always felt unimportant to them. When I was in high school and college, my parents didn't have time for me because they were building their business. I basically raised myself from the ninth grade on. By the time I started my career, got married, and started a family, Mom and Dad's business had become extremely successful and took even more of their time. Then, because of some health problems, they had to sell the business and retire. I think at that point they began to see things through different eyes. They began to take an interest in me and my family. It's as if they wanted to make up for lost time. Rebuilding relationships became just as important as projecting profits once had been. It's too bad it had to happen so late in life, but at least it happened. And all this has taught me the importance of actively taking an interest in my child's life and world at every stage."

If you want understanding, try giving some.
—Malcolm Forbes

The take-away for you and me? Start talking, listening, and seeking to understand. It's never too late to start building a bridge between the generations. The ball is in our court.

2
Prepare Kids Well for the Big World

Come to the edge, He said. They said: we are afraid.
Come to the edge, He said. They came. He pushed
them, and they flew.
—Guillaume Apollinaire
(1880–1918)

*V*irginia Satir, author of *The New Peoplemaking*, summed up
our job as parents succinctly: "To me, this is the end point
of the bringing up of children—that they become autonomous,
independent, creative people who are now peers to the people
who introduced them into the world." Isn't that every parent's
goal? We long for our children to grow into wise, healthy, contributing adults who make the world a better place through their
responsible behavior and creativity. To that end we've got to prepare them for launch, get them ready to handle the often cold
and cruel world. There's much we can do to make our children's
entry into independence as smooth and uneventful as possible.

TIME TO RISK AND RELEASE

It's impossible to launch children into the world to live on
their own without risk taking—yours and theirs. When they
were young, there were football teams to play on, first dates to

go on, and—the daddy of them all (excuse the pun)—learning to drive a car. With a little faith (and sometimes a lot of nail biting), we survived those unnerving firsts that steeled us for the bigger challenges we now face.

Never bend your head. Always hold it high. Look the world straight in the eye.

—Helen Keller

As new parents, we read child-raising books by the experts so that we would know the skills we could teach our new baby at various ages and stages: to speak, to eat with a spoon, to use the "big potty" (always a day of celebration). It's easy to forget when children get older and, as if it happened overnight, are taller than us that we should still be training them. Parenting, contrary to kids' wishes, doesn't stop when they enter high school. We still keep teaching and training, and although they think they know it all, they don't.

Just as we wouldn't send children out to ride a bicycle to school without giving them training on the rules of the road and proper gear, we shouldn't expect our children to know how to get along in the world. Whether our children go off to college, trade school, or the military or take a few years off to work or explore the world, they'll be making many decisions for the first time—and living with the consequences of those decisions. Schools rarely teach the important life skills—caring for and maintaining belongings, setting personal boundaries wisely, handling money—that kids need before they leave home.

Before your children pack their bags and head for the big city, there are some important things they should know. The time and effort you spend preparing them for life on their own will go a long way toward helping them make wise choices and cope capably with the inevitable mishaps and crises of life. We want them to be successful adults; therefore we need to help them learn to manage the nitty-gritty issues of life.

[Autonomy] is freedom to develop one's self—to increase one's knowledge, improve one's skills, and achieve responsibility for one's conduct. And it is freedom to live one's own life, to choose among alternative courses of action so long as no injury to others results.
—Thomas S. Ssasz

In Chapter 10, you will find a lot of ideas on how to prepare your child for practical concerns. In the present chapter, we will look at two important issues for which our children need to be personally prepared: boundaries and independence. In other words, as they move toward independence and autonomy, they need to know where to draw the line and who's going to draw it.

RITE OF PASSAGE

Although many cultures in the world honor a child's "graduation" into adulthood through rite-of-passage ceremonies, in our country we tend to ignore the event. This means we fail to signal to a child that he or she is now an adult, entitled to all the benefits and responsibilities thereof.

We can do better: We can create a ceremony that initiates our children into grown-up life with memory-making festivity and life-changing confidence. A good "graduation" will do the following:

- Tell the child you value him or her. You respect his or her dignity as an adult human being.

- Utilize a symbol. A retiree earns a gold watch. In your family, what should a newborn adult receive?

- Reflect an investment of consideration, planning, and finances. This is worth doing right.

- Do more than celebrate the moment. It will inspire your child to go forth with expectation.

SETTING PERSONAL BOUNDARIES

By the time your kids leave home, one hopes they have internalized a code of ethics and drawn their moral boundaries. Whether you feel their standards are firmly anchored or still a little fuzzy, it's a good idea to talk about this important issue.

Those who would be free must be virtuous.
—Clinton Rossiter

Make it a priority to schedule some time before they leave to ask your children to describe the personal guidelines they have set for themselves for when they are out on their own. If they don't know how to verbalize their answers, you can help them out by presenting some scenarios in which they could find themselves faced with hard decisions. For example, ask your children how they would respond in the following situations:

- You learn that a friend or your roommate is selling drugs.

- You find out it's commonplace to cheat on tests or falsify expense reports.

- You are date raped.

- You are asked to do something unlawful as part of a social organization's initiation.

- You are at a party that's getting out of hand. Alcohol is flowing freely, and you begin to question the safety of the people at the party, including yourself.

- You are offered an opportunity to make a lot of money doing something that goes against your conscience.

- You have the opportunity to get a false ID.

- You learn a simple way to cheat on your income taxes.

Tis easier to prevent bad habits than to break them.
—Benjamin Franklin

When your young adult faces a tough choice, the fact that he's thought through the situation beforehand doesn't guarantee a better response, but it will make it easier for him to make a wise decision. And remember, you know your child better than anyone else does, sometimes even better than she knows herself. Every human being has "blind spots," the black holes of life people get sucked into because of their personalities, natural tendencies, or upbringing. Maybe you've never thought about it in this way, but you probably have noticed some of your child's black-hole tendencies from a very young age.

Have you ever said something like this: "My daughter's known how to get her way since she was three years old" or "My son has tried to bend the rules since day one"? As innocent as these tendencies may seem, they are potential black holes. By helping your child anticipate some of the challenges he may face, you can help him develop the wisdom and self-discipline to step away when tempted to do things that don't reflect his values.

THE ISSUE OF AUTHORITY

Maybe now you and your young adult have had a chance to discuss or at least schedule some time to talk about boundaries and authority. These are important topics, but there's another issue to consider when an older child takes the first step toward independence: living away from home. Parents and children alike wonder how much sway and say parents should still have over a child's life. If you're wondering about this, there's a question you can ask to bring some clarity to the issue: Whose dime is he or she on?

If it is not addressed and understood by parent and child, this simple question can cause great resentment and relational rifts for years to come. If you are paying for your child's education or in some way providing support to an older child, you still have some degree of authority over the child's life. But remember this: It is critically important to state your guidelines and expectations clearly while you're still paying, along with the consequences of not adhering to the standards on which you, your spouse, and your child agree.

I often meet parents who don't require older children to adhere to agreed-upon guidelines. They turn their heads when their sons or daughters are ticketed for DWI, can't seem to make it to classes that begin before noon, or ask to borrow money again and again without paying back prior loans as they promised. By living in denial, these parents are not doing their children any favors.

A college professor approached me recently after a speaking engagement. I had mentioned the topic of this book in my speech, and she told me how she struggles with students who don't do assignments but still think their grades should be good. "But even worse," she commented, "are the parents who call and want me to give good grades to their kids even though they're not doing the work." Sounds unimaginable, doesn't it?

Who, then, is free? The man who can govern himself.
—Horace

There's something every parent needs to understand clearly: If we want to launch mature, responsible adults into the world, there are times during the transition period from dependence to independence when we must stand firm for the good of the child and his or her future. If a child, no matter how old, is still receiving support from her parents and does not fulfill her responsibilities—to obey the law, attend classes, pay for certain expenses, whatever—she should not be rewarded, which in some cases simply means continuing to enjoy various privileges. To deny our children the experience of suffering consequences is to do them a great disservice.

Think about it: When our kids get real jobs in the real world and are out on their own, if they don't fulfill their responsibilities, they won't have the privilege of getting a paycheck or even keeping a job. It's not easy, but it's true—and it's an important way we show love for our children. We do them a huge favor when we help them make the critical connection between privileges and responsibility—before the stakes are higher and the falls are harder.

COMING TO TERMS

There's one strategy that has helped the members of our family know what we can expect from each other, defuse arguments, and live for the most part in peace and harmony with each other. It's a simple equation people use in business every day, and it works in families as well: C + N = E. Here's the gist of it.

Take the example of buying a house. You have two people (buyer and seller) who each have desires and opinions. The seller communicates his desire to be paid a certain amount of money, and the buyer communicates her desire to pay a smaller amount of money. After each party *communicates* what he or she would like to see happen, they *negotiate* their way to some middle ground they feel they both can live with and then come up with some *expectations* that they write into a contract and sign.

Now apply the same strategy to coming up with expectations for an older child. Perhaps you *communicate* with your child some things you want to see happen, such as a B+ average at the end of the semester and no extra charges on her cell-phone bill. Then you allow your child to *communicate* her desires and opinions. Maybe she says she'll try to maintain a B+ average, but she brings up the fact that she's taking some harder than usual classes this semester and a C average might be more realistic. As for her cell-phone bill, she reminds you that her boyfriend lives in another state, and since they like to keep in touch, she would be willing to pay for the extra minutes. You both give a little on your positions—*negotiate*—and decide on some *expectations* you can live with. Whether you put your terms on paper is up to you, but it's not a bad idea so that you can refer to them later and your child won't be able to use as an excuse "I didn't know I wasn't supposed to do that."

I count him braver who overcomes his desires than him who conquers his enemies; the hardest victory is the victory over self.
                                                —Aristotle

If you decide to write a simple contract, you might start by asking what your child sees as his responsibility to you and himself. Then talk about what is and isn't acceptable behavior. Also keep in mind that "talk about" means just that. Make sure it's a two-way conversation. Although there will be some issues on which you can't and shouldn't budge, watch your tone. A child (or an adult, for that matter) will always receive a loving admonition better than a dictum from an autocratic ruler on high.

A stumble may prevent a fall.
                                                —Thomas Fuller

---

Here are a few sample points you might want to adapt to your own family as you develop your own set of agreed-upon guidelines for a contract with an older child:

- I understand my parents have the final say while they are paying my way.

- I will exercise responsibility with my time. Grades come before privileges, and so I will attend classes and faithfully fulfill course requirements.

- I will express my freedom responsibly. I will try to make wise decisions.

- I will treat my body and everyone else's with deep respect.

- I agree to be truthful in all things.

- I understand that having belongings is a privilege, not a right, and so I will take care of my possessions and respect others' property as well.

THE TALE OF TWO FAMILIES

I want to tell you the stories of two young adults who are probably much like your children and mine. The mistakes these young adults made probably are the kind our children will make—if they haven't already—at some point. These young adults have parents who love them just as much as you and I love our children, but they responded in very different ways to the mistakes their children made in their transitional years. I learned an important truth from each story. I think you will, too.

Will's Story

William and Dotty, the parents of a thirty-two-year-old son, Will, shared with me how their failure to stand firm on the expectations they set for their son caused a great deal of heartache for both them and their son for years to come. When Will went away to college, they gave him one of their credit cards for certain school expenses and emergencies. It was understood that Will would get a part-time job close to campus to pay for his social life and entertainment.

Like many young adults, Will learned that a credit card is a very convenient way to pay for things, and since the bill went each month to his parents' mailbox, he didn't have a clue about how much he was spending. After the first month of school the bill showed $500 worth of miscellaneous expenditures. William and Dotty questioned Will about the charges, but they let the incident pass with a simple request to "hold down the spending."

The next month their bill detailed more than $700 in charges. They talked to Will about getting a part-time job, but he replied that he was too busy with school and the surrounding activities (read: parties and weekend trips to the beach). Month after month William wrote the check to the credit card company and bailed Will out of his part of the agreed-upon arrangement. He never "held Will's feet to the fire," as William put it. The regular bailout became an expected routine for Will month after month, year after year.

During Will's senior year the payments became a real burden and a financial threat to William and Dotty. They had to dip into their retirement fund to make ends meet each month. They tried to put their foot down, say no, and stop the destructive, irresponsible pattern. When confronted, Will became angry and spewed words of resentment. Not being people who were comfortable with conflict, William and Dotty caved in to Will again and again.

Don't handicap your children by making their lives easy.
—Robert A. Heinlein

Ten years later, in his early thirties, having run up his parents' card to the limit years earlier and maxed out his own cards, Will came to his parents again for money to pay his rent—or else he would be out on the street. This time William and Dotty wisely said they would work to help him get on his feet, but only if he agreed to go with them to sessions with a family therapist.

After a few weeks of counseling, Will began making some headway at getting out of debt and breaking the stranglehold of irresponsible spending in his life. "He's not out of the woods yet," William concluded with compassion and hope, "but he's on his way."

The lesson for you and me? Standing firm with our kids early on can save us a lot of pain later on.

Drew's Story

Last May Bill and I received a college graduation invitation from the son of some longtime friends. Drew's graduation was an especially significant occasion because many people close to the family wondered if this young man would ever move from partying to "pomp and circumstance." When he was a freshman, Drew's parents sent him off in a nice car to a prominent university, where he soon decided that drinking was more fun than studying. By the end of the first semester he had totaled his car and flunked out of school.

He has seen but half the universe who has not been shown the house of pain.

—Ralph Waldo Emerson

Drew's parents, of course, were not pleased—to put it mildly. A whole semester's tuition was down the drain because their son had not taken school seriously, plus he had been an irresponsible driver in what could have been a fatal accident. In response, here's what Drew's parents did.

First, they expressed their unconditional love for Drew but explained that wanting what was best for him meant helping him learn the lessons of his choices. Second, they had him come back home to live with them, get a hard-labor job during the spring and summer semesters, and save the money he made to start paying back the tuition he'd squandered. Any money remaining he was to use toward the down payment on another car.

Sound harsh?

Fast-forward to the beginning of the fall semester. After eight months Drew had saved enough to repay his parents the wasted tuition, buy a car (a far less exciting car than the one his parents had given him), and return to school. Then—hold on to your hat, this is a true story—his parents gave him, in one lump sum, all the money they had saved over the years to send him to college. (Pretty risky, I'd say.) They told Drew that they hoped he'd use it for his education, but it was his to do with as he wanted. If he spent it on something besides college, that was his choice. And if he ran out, then too bad: He'd be on his own.

Failure is God's own tool for carving some of the finest outlines in the character of his children.

—Thomas Hodgkin

After eight months of hard work, no car, and being away from his friends at school, this young man evidently had learned a good lesson. Life took on a new perspective. Reality had set in. Drew carefully managed the money his parents had given him. He got a part-time job on his own initiative near campus, invested some of the money they'd given him in the stock market (it was better a few years ago) so that it grew in value, and ended up graduating with honors.

This couple wisely handled their son's mistakes. They loved him but let him experience real-life consequences when he failed to make good choices. Many times being a winner means learning important lessons from losing.

If we don't discipline ourselves the world will do it for us.
—William Feather

SERIOUS SITUATIONS

When our children were toddlers, we were ready to move into action immediately if they ran out into the street. But what should we do if we see an adult child in a dangerous or life-threatening situation, such as dependence on drugs or alcohol, prolonged depression, or living with an abusive partner? If our children ask for help, that's one thing. But what if they don't ask for help or even tell us to stay out of their business?

If a grown child has a problem you think could be life-threatening, seek help—*now*. Recognize that you cannot solve your child's problems and that if you try to carry all the responsibility yourself for helping the child, you will only make things worse. Pick up the phone and call a local church or synagogue and ask for resources. Find the hot lines, hospitals, law enforcement officials, support groups, physicians, and others with expertise in the problem with which you're dealing.

Seek immediate help if any of the following describe your adult child:

- Talking about death, suicide, or lost hope or saying that life seems unbearable

- Talking about killing or hurting someone else

- Showing severe depression—crying, not eating, sleeping, or dressing; neglecting normal activities; acting lethargic and uncommunicative

- Showing unexplained injuries, bruises, or broken bones

- Mistreating or ignoring the survival needs of a spouse or child

- Revealing dangerous drug or alcohol abuse

Freedom is not only the absence of external restraints. It also is the absence of irresistible internal compulsions, unmanageable passions, and uncensorable appetites. From the need to resist, manage, and censor the passions there flows the need to do so in the interest of some ends rather than others. Hence freedom requires reflective choice about life.

—George Will

WHO'S GOING TO CALL THE SHOTS?

Let's face it: for many years in our children's lives, we called all of (or at least most of) the shots. We protected them from injury and disappointment by making good decisions for them: "Don't run by the pool." "Don't cross the road without me." "Don't pet every dog you meet—one might be dangerous." It's a hard habit to break. Maybe the toughest job of every parent with a young adult in the transition from dependence to independence is to know how to respond and help a child learn from the mistakes he or she makes along the way.

As you begin to let your child call more of the shots for herself or himself, you are doing more than making your job as a parent easier. You are expressing your faith in your child, which goes many miles toward making him or her a confident and wise adult. Learning to let kids grow into and express their adulthood—as well as facing the consequences of childish choices—is an investment that will pay off for years to come. As always, communication is the key, and love lights the way.

As you prepare your kids for launch into the galaxy of college, jobs, marriage, and parenting, keep in mind that your efforts at making the entry smooth must be matched by your kids' willingness to heed wise counsel. Most will listen more than they let on; many will be grateful beyond words once they realize just how tough the real world can be. Keep an affectionate light burning in the window, and let your kids fly; this is the moment you've all been waiting and working for. Godspeed!

3

Mend Broken Fences and Love in Ways That Matter

To love others is not enough! Somehow we must make them feel that love, because the only kind of love we can use is the love we can feel.
—David Jeremiah

*I*n the film *Dances with Wolves* Lieutenant John Dunbar comes upon a burned-up covered wagon on the plains with the skeleton of a pioneer lying nearby. His traveling companion comments, "Someone back east is wondering, 'Now why don't he write?'" Since written communication is out of vogue, most parents today aren't waiting for a letter, but I know a lot of mothers and fathers who wonder, "Why doesn't he call?"

The reasons are as varied as our children themselves, but a major cause for noncommunication may simply be hurt. As hard as we work at being good parents, we all, without exception, fail at one time or another. It's just possible that one of our failures ignited a pain large enough to create a relational rift between us and our children.

The great news is that almost every rift can be repaired. If you know that significant issues have been allowed to fester for years or even if you feel that your relationship is fine but still lack an easy give-and-take with your kids, you can take some steps to start the repair work needed to get things flowing once again.

Little children disturb your sleep; big ones your life.
—Yiddish saying

THREE TOOLS FOR REPAIRING RELATIONSHIPS

1. Take the Initiative

Even if you have what seems to be a good relationship with your older offspring, it might be healthy to ask them if they are carrying wounds from the past. Often we hurt our children unknowingly and they bear the scars into adulthood. It might have been something we did or something we failed to do. Whatever the case, we don't want them carrying a needless burden in their lives.

Last Thanksgiving we were all together for the holidays, and my husband broached this subject with our boys. He did it in a conversation over dinner at the end of a discussion about all our personal dreams and aspirations. He simply said that one of his dreams was that we would continue to be a close family through the years, and if we (the parents) had hurt them in any way that was yet to be resolved, he didn't want that holding them back or cooling our relationship.

Their responses at the dinner table were lighthearted. "Dad, I remember when I was six, you wouldn't let me put another teaspoon of sugar on my soggy cereal and made me eat it anyway, I almost threw up." "Mom, I can't believe how much easier you are on James; he gets away with things I never got away with." But in more private moments the boys shared some hurts they still remembered. We listened rather than defended, talked about the surrounding circumstances, and asked for their forgiveness.

2. Take Responsibility

As the older and presumably wiser member of the family, you should own your part of the hurt, however small it seems to you. Chances are that your son or daughter will never be able to own his or her responsibility until you accept yours.

Here are some tips for confronting conflict with an older child in ways that say "I'm ready to hear and admit my part."

- Make no assumptions about your child's thoughts or emotions. Ask questions to get accurate information.

- Make sure you do less talking than your child does.

- Maintain eye contact throughout the conversation.

- Don't act as a judge; act as a compassionate friend.

- Don't tackle more than one problem at a time. Leave previous conflicts for other conversations.

- Let your child take her or his time. Don't rush.

- Avoid the words *always* and *never*. Accusations just make people defensive.

- Spend more energy on hearing what your child is really saying than on making sure your child hears you.

- Keep focused on the child's behavior; don't veer off into calling names, attacking the child's character, or blaming.

- If you're confused, say so.

- Don't accuse by starting sentences with "You . . ." Instead, describe your feelings with "I . . ."

- Occasionally repeat what your child is saying to make sure you've heard him or her: "So you felt resentment when this occurred."

- Let your children express their feelings and don't condemn them even if they seem unreasonable to you.

- Don't expect your child to respond to conflicts the way you do. There is no "normal."

- Be sensitive to the feelings behind the words.

- If anger is near the boiling point, pause for a few minutes before continuing the conversation.

- Remember that your aim is to reach an understanding, not "win" an argument.

- Show respect: no eye rolling, sighing, or shrugging.

- Consider your part of the conflict and what actions *you* can take to resolve it.

3. Seek Forgiveness

If you come to realize that you've hurt your children by something you did or didn't do, begin making it right by asking their forgiveness for the mistake you made. Whether it was intentional is immaterial.

And if on consideration, one can find no faults on one's own side, then cry for mercy; for this must be a most dangerous delusion.

—C. S. Lewis

We have practiced this open admission of wrongdoing and confession with each other and our boys for almost thirty years and have seen its positive impact. An unqualified humble confession of offense is powerful in any relationship. Here are the things we've learned about asking forgiveness.

Find the right time. Timing is crucial. Make sure you have enough time to talk uninterruptedly, in private. Allow time for the other person to reflect and respond by sharing his or her hurt.

Make it unconditional. Avoid the word *if.* Don't say, "*If* I've hurt you" or "*If* I've done this." Don't mix blame with your confession. This is difficult, because every offense has a context. You may have been provoked, but that is not the issue. Focus on your part of the offense even if it was only 10 percent of the story. Simply say, "I did *this*. I was wrong. I'm sorry. Would you please forgive me." Then wait for his or her response.

Be prepared for a negative response. Opening up an old wound is often painful, so be prepared at first for a response you don't want. Don't get angry or you will reveal that you really don't feel you were wrong in the first place. Forgiveness is never something we deserve. It is something that another person graciously offers to us.

People who fight fire with fire usually end up with ashes.
—Abigail Van Buren

Offer to make it right. Many things we do to our children innocently or intentionally are things we cannot undo. Your willingness to do what it takes to make things right, whether trying to reconcile with other family members or just demonstrating your willingness to change over time, may be what moves them to forgive you.

Don't expect your child to change. Make sure you don't demand that your son or daughter's behavior change toward you. Your child may need time to see that you, the one who caused the pain, have changed. Forgiveness does not mean that you automatically get to return to the place you once occupied in his or her life. For example, if you violated trust, forgiveness does not mean that trust is restored. Trust is something that is built, and you must show the other person that you are trustworthy once again and have dealt with the inner issues that made you untrustworthy to begin with.

He that won't be counseled can't be helped.
—Benjamin Franklin

Seek counsel for the issues you can't unravel. Sometimes, especially with family, relationships that have been left to sour over time are almost impossible to revive without professional help. If you have reached that point, for the sake of the most important relationships in your life, get some help from a family counselor. Ideally, both parties should go, but if your son or daughter refuses, take the responsibility to get all the help you can.

STARTING OVER: MAKING COMMUNICATION A PRIORITY

Once you've started rebuilding your bridges with your son or daughter, some new methods of staying—or getting—in touch are in order. To keep your renewed relationship on the right track, consider these suggestions.

Do It on Their Terms

It's important for parents to establish communication on their son or daughter's ground. It's our job to communicate in ways that make them want to keep in contact, that is, to conform to them, not make them conform to us. One of the ways we can do this is by using e-mail. This is a comfortable and easy method of communication for our boys, and so it's the one we use the most. Bill and I communicate almost daily about something with our sons by e-mail. We ask questions and pass on information, jokes, and bits of wisdom to each other.

The first duty of love is to listen.
—Paul Tillich

One of my peeves about many older mothers I meet is that they won't learn how to use a computer—a central part of a young adult's life. Maybe our kids would keep in touch more if we communicated the way they do. Moms' reluctance reminds me of how my grandmother wouldn't have anything to do with automobiles when they became available to the masses. In her mind, she had always ridden the bus and that was fine for her. How many more times would we have been able to see her if she had been able to drive to see us?

Make It About Them, Not About Us

We all have a lot of wisdom to pass on to our sons and daughters, but if they sense that the conversation is more about us than about them, they are likely to begin to avoid communicating with us. One son I know used to avoid calls from his father because the experience was so deflating to him. The son was going through a significant financial struggle. At first he appreciated his father's frequent calls, but pretty soon it became evident why the father was calling. He was anxious for his son and was hoping for good news to make himself feel better. He was calling to relieve his own anxiety, not to help his son. The calls turned into sessions in which the father would pummel the son with questions he couldn't answer, leading the son to feel more troubled than he had been before the call.

> *A low self-love in the parent desires that his child should repeat his character and fortune. . . . I suffer whenever I see that common sight of a parent or senior imposing his opinion and way of thinking and being on a young soul to which they are totally unfit. Cannot we let people be themselves, and enjoy life in their own way? You are trying to make another you. One's enough.*
>
> —Ralph Waldo Emerson

When our children are going through a difficult time, we need to listen, encourage, and give good advice—sparingly and only when asked. Most of all, they need to know we believe in them, not feel our concern as we worry about their future.

Watch the Negatives

If at all possible, try to deal with negative issues face to face. Communication involves not only words but also tone of voice and body language. Interestingly, words alone contribute only 7 percent of total communication; this is why letters and especially terse e-mails are so easily misunderstood. In a phone conversation you add tone of voice, which contributes 38 percent to understanding, but if you're not face to face, you lose 55 percent of what you want to communicate to someone else. When you are talking about something difficult, you need to have everything working for effective communication.

My husband and I got caller ID put on our phone. This way we know when it's his parents calling. I know that sounds crazy, but we want to talk to them only when we feel emotionally up for it. They are always giving advice we didn't ask for and criticizing us for something. We don't call them much for the same reason. It's sad. I know that they have a lot we could learn from them, and when we have children, I'll want them to spend time with their parents. I just wish they'd be more positive and encouraging. I don't think that's too much to ask.

—Beth, age 26

Allow Some Time for Healing

After your heartfelt attempts to correct any wrongs you've done, if your child is still reluctant to communicate often or openly, don't assume that you've failed or that the relationship is hopeless. Human beings need lots of time to process information and feelings. It may take weeks or months for your child to feel "safe" enough to develop a new relationship with you. Give him the time he needs; don't push, demand, or rage. As you demonstrate your love consistently and over time, your actions will speak for themselves.

Man does not live by words alone, despite the fact that sometimes he has to eat them.
                                          —Adlai Stevenson

Remember that the privilege of a strong relationship with your child is something the child can choose to give—or not. You can't force friendly feelings. But keep doing your part and give your child respectful time to size up your intentions.

WHAT LOVE LANGUAGE DO YOU SPEAK?

Whether your relationship with your adult child is strained or comfortable, you still may need a refresher course on communicating your love effectively. Years ago Bill and I read Dr. Gary Chapman's book *The Five Love Languages* and were surprised to learn that not everyone feels love the same way. What warms one person's heart will not necessarily do the same for another: Love is not a "one size fits all" emotion. According to Dr. Chapman, each person has a primary love language that especially communicates love to him or her. Your child will feel most loved through one of these means: hearing words of affirmation, receiving gifts or acts of service, spending quality time with you, or feeling your physical touch. Thus, your child may not sense your love if you are expressing it in a "language" she doesn't understand.

[Love] both gives and receives, and in giving it receives.
—Thomas Merton

It is the parents' *job* to know the primary love languages of their children, no matter what age, and deliver affection in that lingo. Observe your children. Watch how they express love to others. That is a clue to their love language. Take note of the things they request of you. Many times their requests will be in keeping with their own love language. Notice the things for which they are most appreciative. Those things are also likely indicators of their primary love language.

I haven't met a parent yet who doesn't love his or her children sincerely, but I've met thousands of parents who have failed to communicate love in the proper language, and so their children have empty emotional tanks. Fortunately, it's never too late to express love in ways that make a lasting impression on your children.

HOW YOUNG ADULTS FEEL LOVED

It's been said that we don't know the love our parents had for us until we have children of our own. Perhaps as parents we can improve on that—actually show the love we feel in ways our young adults can understand before they create progeny of their own. Here's how fifty young adults responded to the question "Now that you're an adult, what are some things your parents do that make you feel loved?"

1. Now that I work in the same world as my dad, I appreciate his not calling me by my nickname.

2. My parents set a good example for me of how a loving marriage works.

3. Even though I didn't like it at the time, I'm glad my parents made me do chores. I know how to clean my own apartment.

4. My parents keep our child once a week so that my husband and I can go out on a date.

5. My mom lets me explain my point of view without criticizing me.

6. My parents don't push me to get a job that pays more money. They understand that it's really important that I like my work.

7. My mother left my room just the way it was when I went away to college.

8. When I graduated from college, my dad wrote a letter to me telling me how much he loved me and believed in my future. I saved the letter.

9. When I was in high school, my dad started taking me on a yearly fly-fishing trip. I'm thirty now, and we still do it.

10. My mom hired a maid service to clean up my condo once a month. She knows I'm really busy with my job and don't have time to do it. It's a simple gift that means a lot to me.

11. When I come back home to visit, my mom fixes a lot of food and encourages me to have my old friends over to the house. She makes it easier for me to maintain relationships with people I care about.

12. My parents don't support us, but they'll pay for extra educational opportunities for my kids, such as piano lessons and summer camp.

13. My brothers and sisters live all over the country. My parents go to a lot of trouble to make sure we stay connected. They set up a family Web page where we can keep up with each other's lives and post pictures.

14. When I got married, my dad gave me some good tips about sex. I think his advice has helped my wife and me avoid some problems in that area.

15. When I decided to take a career path different from the one my father had hoped for, he gave me his blessing anyway.

16. My parents rent a big house at the beach every summer and invite us and my sister's family to spend a week.

17. My mom learned to do e-mail so that we could "talk" every day.

18. My parents are a great sounding board. They take the time to listen to my ideas and give me wise counsel.

19. I like hearing from my parents' friends that my parents have said nice things about me.

20. My parents give us thoughtful gifts at Christmas. They give us things on our list but also listen throughout the year for hints about things we might like to have.

21. My parents let the past be the past. They never bring up the times I disappointed them.

22. My mom created a costume closet at her house for my kids. They love to go over to her house and play dress-up.

23. My dad slips a twenty-dollar bill in my hand every time I leave his house.

24. My parents make my wife feel loved.

25. When my mom comes to stay at our house, she cooks up a lot of meals and puts them in the freezer. This is such a big help to me.

26. I could have shipped my stuff, but my parents rented a U-Haul truck and drove 1,200 miles when I went away to college.

27. When my dad comes to visit, he helps me with things that need fixing around the house.

28. My parents remind me that they pray for me every day.

29. When my wife and I have to figure out whose family we're going to stay with during the holidays, my parents tell us to do what's best for *us*. They don't pressure us to stay with them.

30. When I graduated from college, my dad helped me create a budget and set up accounting software on my computer.

31. My dad is a good role model for me about what it means to be a successful businessman and an honest businessman at the same time.

32. My parents loved me through a really hard time in my life. I made some bad decisions that I know disappointed them, but I never doubted their love.

33. My mom sends me care packages at my dorm.

34. My dad treats me like a peer, not a child.

35. My parents don't bug me about getting married. I'm just not ready.

36. My parents got an 800 number at their house so that my brother and I can call home anytime we want.

37. When I go back home, my mom gives me a foot massage just like she used to do after football practice.

38. After their divorce, my parents never spoke negatively about each other in front of me or my sister.

39. Although my mother has remarried, she is sensitive about my desire to see my dad.

40. My parents paid for me to see a counselor after my divorce.

41. My father points out things that I'm doing well.

42. Every time I call home, my parents tell me they are proud of me.

43. My parents instilled in me a really strong work ethic.

44. My parents encouraged me to save my body for the woman I marry. There were plenty of times I didn't want to, but I'm glad I did.

45. My mom and dad don't interfere when I have to discipline my child.

46. My parents are fun to be with. I don't think I really appreciated this until I began hearing stories from coworkers about how they hate to go home.

47. My mom stops what she's doing and looks me in the eye when I'm talking to her.

48. My parents have gone out of their way to love and accept my new wife and stepchildren.

49. My dad helps me work on my car when I come home.

50. My parents remind me that they pray for me every day. This means a lot to me.

SHOWING TRUST CAN DEMONSTRATE LOVE

Giving an adult child a job or a responsibility that shows your trust can translate into showing your love in the minds of some children. This might be something as small as asking your son to speak at your Rotary Club. Or it might be something as big as what my mom did when I was twenty-five and my sister was twenty-one. My mother owned retail clothing stores and went on buying trips to New York and Dallas five times a year. Just before one of her trips she had to have emergency surgery. She assigned my sister and me the job of going to market and buying merchandise for that spring. This meant we'd be spending a lot of money and having to make many decisions about styles, colors, and sizes. Rather than being overwhelmed by the responsibility, I felt ten feet tall. Just the fact that Mom entrusted something so important to us meant the world. We worked hard, did our best, and made some good decisions and some bad decisions. As I look back on it, the trip probably cost Mom a lot of money in leftover sale merchandise that we hadn't made such a good call on, but she never complained or criticized. And it definitely built my relationship with her as well as my confidence in myself.

LOVING CAN BE HARD TO DO

Of course, there are times when children can be downright unlovable and loving them is painful. Maybe the problem is a child's recurring brushes with the law, the personal disappointment you feel when your son consistently accomplishes less than he's capable of, or just a coolness between you and your adult child that drains your energy every time you talk. Here are seven guiding principles for clearing clogged communication lines—and reestablishing the language of love—with your child, no matter how difficult the problem.

1. Respond Thoughtfully Instead of Reacting Emotionally

Be aware that every situation presents us with a choice that will either enhance or inhibit positive communication. In a way, each encounter is a defining moment, because relationships are never static; they are dynamic and are moving in a healthy or a destructive direction. Sages throughout the ages have said, "We are a product of our choices, not of our circumstances." In whatever words you put it, it's important to realize that we have choices about how we relate to our children—even when they have related poorly with us—and those choices have effects.

Many waters cannot quench love, neither can floods drown it.
—Song of Solomon 8:7

For example, when a son tells you he's quitting his well-paying job (the one he got as a result of the expensive education you paid for), buying an old van, and moving cross-country to Aspen to "find himself," take a minute to put emotion aside. Think what you would want and need to hear from a parent if you were in the same situation.

2. Keep Things in Perspective

Blowing things out of proportion can happen easily and unintentionally, resulting in a larger than necessary conflict. Like many other moms I know, I have an enlarging machine in my mind. (Although you won't find a picture of such a machine in medical books, it does exist.) The enlarger operates at all hours of the day but seems to be most active at night. That's when I lie awake reviewing situations such as a remark about a meal I cooked that hit me the wrong way. Then, with the help of my machine, I make the fairly insignificant occurrence into a scene from a soap opera: "I am never going to cook again. Nobody appreciates the time I slave in the kitchen. See if I invite him and his friends over for dinner again."

When the enlarging machine is at work, the last thing we think of doing is responding calmly and creatively by finding out what food he would like better, suggesting a team approach to cooking so that everyone gets the meals he likes occasionally, or scheduling a family potluck in which everyone contributes to the meal and commits to keeping his comments to himself. The fact is, we have the power to choose how we'll look at/respond to perceived comments and the like.

The mind is its own place, and in itself can make a heaven of hell, a hell of heaven.

—John Milton

An up side of growing older is the wisdom that only comes with years. When I was a young mother, I remember likening my ability to cope with life to the Plimsoll line on a ship. (This is the line on the hull of a ship that shows the depth to which it can be loaded.) Some days the smallest incidents would trigger the enlarging machine in my mind, which made me feel as if I was overloaded and quickly sinking. For years, it didn't dawn on me that I had the power to choose how I would respond.

The older I get, the more I realize how little control I have over life's circumstances—and other people. But I do have control over what I choose to focus on, and that greatly affects my attitude and my ability to solve the problem.

—Phyllis, age 64

With age comes experience and perspective. I can't say that my enlarging machine is completely out of commission, but it definitely doesn't see as much action as it once did. Things that once seemed like mountains, now look more like molehills. It's easier to see how small incidents that rub me the wrong way pale into insignificance next to the real critical issues of life. So what if I don't feel appreciated for cooking dinner? At least we're eating, and eating well compared to the majority of the world. At the right time I'll bring up the subject in a nonemotional way and talk about the importance of appreciating what we do for each other.

3. Think the Best

In our country we abide by a law that states that a person is innocent until proved guilty. That's a good strategy in a family, too. If my schedule is packed and I've asked one of the boys to run an errand and he forgets, I can immediately start thinking he doesn't care, he's irresponsible, and I've been a terrible mother in raising him. That can build into anger that he doesn't appreciate me for all I've done, and the emotions spiral downward from there.

Whatever is true, whatever is honorable, whatever is right, whatever is pure, whatever is lovely, whatever is of good repute, if there is any excellence and if anything is worthy of praise, let your mind dwell on these things.
—Philippians 4:8

All I really need to do is start thinking the best of him and ask if something came up that kept him from doing the errand. Maybe his car overheated, or maybe he just forgot. At any rate, my going ballistic is nothing but destructive; it just causes an explosion from which we all have to recover.

It doesn't hurt to be optimistic. You can always cry later.
—Lucimar Santos de Lima

In a more dramatic example, a friend told us about the time her nineteen-year-old daughter came home from college not feeling well, so the mom took her to the doctor. The doctor's office ran a routine pregnancy test, which came out positive. The daughter swore to her mother that she had not had sexual relations with her boyfriend and she couldn't be pregnant. This wise mother decided to believe the best of her daughter, and she told the doctor the test must be wrong because her daughter said so. She risked looking foolish and gullible, but she asked the doctor to run another test, and guess what? It was negative. The first one had been a false positive.

This mother's courage and commitments to her daughter helped solidify their relationship. Believing in someone we love keeps communication free and clear.

4. Face the Truth

Even though we want to think the best about our children, there are times we must admit the worst. And on those occasions the problem can seem so overwhelming that we close up and refuse to deal with it by saying, "If I say it's not a problem, it's not," or "It will go away if I ignore it." The trouble is that when we live in denial, we create more of it.

The easiest person to deceive is oneself
—Edward Bulwer-Lytton

For example, your daughter's employer calls you (the emergency contact in her file) to ask if you know why she hasn't been at work the last two days. You fear she's started drinking again. Looking the other way or hoping the situation will clear up by itself is plain old wishful thinking. This situation calls for a loving but firm response. Remind her that you love her unconditionally but do not approve of her behavior. Allow the natural consequences to run their course. Don't "save" her by calling the employer and making up a story about why she's missed work. Help her by getting in touch with a counselor or AA chapter in her area that has experience in dealing with alcohol problems. Be available if you're needed during counseling.

Or maybe you're worried about the friends your son is running around with or the man your daughter married on a whim. Don't take your intuition lightly. Be wise. Watch for warning signs of poor physical or mental health as well as signs of abuse or neglect: lack of motivation, weight loss, problems with eating or sleeping, a drop in grades, drug use, an unexplained injury, serious and persistent conflicts between you and your child, high levels of anxiety or guilt. Seek guidance if you have concerns about these cautionary signals or any other aspect of your young adult's health or behavior. Consult with professors, counselors, religious leaders, or physicians.

Coping with painful situations in a family is very hard; we all know this. But avoiding pain guarantees a shallow family life and unsatisfying relationships with our children—or none at all. Facing the hard truth and seeking to grow from it develop strong character and peaceful, deep relationships. Difficult situations are simply part of life's never-ending curriculum for us and our families.

5. Make Time for What's Most Important

Lack of time is probably the biggest problem for today's busy families. If our calendars are filled until eternity, if we never take time to stop and think, if we're always dealing with interruptions and distractions that call for more attention than they deserve, we'll very likely never change relationships for the better.

Things that matter most must never be at the mercy of things that matter least.

—Goethe

Time is a built-in constraint that we must accept. The fact is, we will never have enough time to do everything we dream of doing. That's why focus and setting priorities are all-important. How vital is mending a relationship with a child you haven't spoken to in a while? How important is it to make sure you can attend Grandparents' Day at your granddaughter's preschool? It's easy to give in to the daily obstacles to affectionate, meaningful relationships with our older children and their children. Maybe it's time we all scrutinized our schedules to see what has become an excuse for letting loved ones slip away. Parental investment of time helps keep families talking.

KIDS FIRST

Making positive relationships with our older children a priority really boils down to *our* choices, and every time we choose a priority, we make our own, and our kids', lives easier. How?

Establishing priorities helps you do the following:

1. Choose opportunities carefully. If you've decided that you'll work on building a quality relationship with your adult son by meeting for golf every Saturday morning, the boss's request that you take work home or meet a client for breakfast on Saturday will be easy to turn down. When a monthy lunch date with your daughter is a priority and a friend calls, asking you to lunch on the same day, ask your friend if you can meet her another day.

We move through life in such a distracted way that we do not even take the time and rest to wonder if any of the things we think, say, or do are worth thinking, saying, or doing.

—Henri J. M. Nouwen

---

2. Focus your time, energy, and resources. When you have to choose between an extra hour at the gym and calling your recently relocated son for a check-in chat, you'll skip the treadmill and let your fingers do the walking instead.

3. Know when to drop activities, and which ones, when you feel overloaded with responsibilities. When your schedule is groaning under its own weight, you choose to drop a community volunteer job rather than "unschedule" after-school baby-sitting for your single-mom daughter.

4. See how added responsibilities will affect the quality of your life in other areas. If taking on a part-time job (and you don't really need the money) means you can't spend any time working with your son on his new business, you opt for helping your son.

5. See the forest when you're lost in the trees. When around the holidays you feel like you're approaching overload, you skip an open house or two and keep your shopping date with your son or daughter.

CUT YOURSELF SOME SLACK

Repeat after me: None of us is perfectly competent, but that's okay. We're human beings and human beings are not perfect. We have all made, and will continue to make, some mistakes. Don't view your child's struggles as your failure. Give yourself credit for all that's gone right in your family; see yourself as a competent parent who's always learning and looking for ways to do a better job. Many moms and dads I meet fear being labeled "bad parents." Maybe at work we're hotshot sales managers, but when it comes to working on relationship issues with our older children, fear of failure cripples us. But if we let fear keep us from responding to our children and building relationships with them, a truly scary thing will result: estrangement, or no relationships at all.

As parents, none of us spells *love* in exactly the same way. But we can all agree that mending relational rifts is essential to keep a relationship growing between us and our adult children. As you take the steps necessary for clear communication, give yourself as much room as you give your children for new feelings of forgiveness and togetherness to take root. Healing always takes time. But you've taken the most important step of all: you've started the process.

4

Be a Dreambuilder,
Not a Dreambuster

*The future belongs to those who believe in the beauty
of their dreams.*
                                        —Eleanor Roosevelt

When kids are little, it's fun to hear their ideas about what they'll grow up to do with their lives. My boys thought being a fireman or an astronaut sounded like great fun. A friend's daughter couldn't settle on just one job, and so at the ripe old age of four she figured she'd just have it all. "I'm going to be a ballerina, clown, and puppeteer," she announced.

We pat their heads and assure them the sky's the limit; we bolster their self-esteem by telling them they are bright enough to become anything they want to be. Helping your children realize their dreams is perhaps the greatest gift you can give them; it's the ultimate act of love.

However, when a teenager boasts about becoming a professional skateboarder or playing bass guitar in a girl band, his or her comments are more worrisome than cute and funny. Our responses to these aspirations may not be so affirming: "Are you nuts? You can't make money doing that. You're going to get a real job. I'm not going to support you for the rest of your life." An accusatory reply like this can cause alienation and the breakdown of a child's self-esteem.

There's a better way. Part of the family mission statement we wrote years ago is to help each other become all that we were created to be. At our house we foster an atmosphere that encourages dreaming. We strive to be dreambuilders, not dreambusters. Like you, I've known many parents who have tried to mold their kids into someone or something *they* think their children should be. It's easy to fall into the trap of pushing a child toward the "right" career, one that offers lots of prestige, pays a lot of money, and provides the most security. When we do this, we're failing to consider our children's unique makeup and the dreams budding within them. Researchers disagree about whether a child is born tabula rasa, a blank slate for us to write on.

Hold fast to dreams, for if dreams die, life is a broken-winged bird that cannot fly.

—Langston Hughes

If you have children, you know the blank-slate theory doesn't hold water. Of course we have an influence on our children, but every parent discovers a clear design in every child that comes prepackaged, ready to be developed. Sometimes parents can be a little too zealous about charting a child's future, with little regard for the unique abilities and motivations of the child. It's our job as parents to help our children discover and pursue their hearts' desires, not ours. Sometimes that takes a great deal of humility.

Something you consider bad may bring out your child's talents; something you consider good may stifle them.

—Chateaubriand

If we were honest, we'd probably all admit there are times we entertain the idea of showing off our children: "Look what I did!" And many of us could confess that we secretly dream that at least one of our children will become a record-breaking Olympic athlete, the head of a multinational corporation, or maybe even president of the United States. Don't get me wrong. Dreaming grand dreams for our children is good, very good, as long as we honor the unique design in each child. This means we must take time to help them look for their strengths, identify their limitations, regard the dreams they recount to us, and respect the unique way they're wired.

> *We can't form our children on our own concepts; we must take them and love them as God gives them to us.*
> —Johann von Goethe

For example, our second-born son has always loved to sell things. In kindergarten Joel enjoyed going door to door selling school fund-raising products; he and his brother started a flower bulb sales business when they were in elementary school; in high school he loved his job at a nursery selling Christmas trees. It should come as no surprise, then, that today he owns his own sales and marketing company. Although his dad and I privately hoped one of our sons would become a physician—the high grades Joel earned in science and math made us think he might be the one—it would not have been right for us to pressure him into going to medical school. If he had become a physician, would he love his job today? I doubt it, unless he could figure out a way to sell products to his patients after an examination, which probably would not be a good thing. No, starting a sales and marketing company is riskier but for him a lot more fun and fulfill-ing, and it's more likely to be the place where he will enjoy success.

Before we understood this concept, we created a lot of miserable moments—for ourselves *and* our firstborn child—

trying to squeeze him into a mold of our making. For example, we dreamed of his playing the piano some day in Carnegie Hall, and so we enrolled him in a preschool music program at a local university and signed him up for private piano lessons. Many an afternoon was ruined as he tried to like this pursuit that was so important to his parents. The problem? John was not meant to be a musician. He does not have excessive amounts of musical talent. It's not surprising, then, that John never envisioned performing on stage.

But John is very artistic; he is a whiz on the computer and has a keen entrepreneurial mind. Years ago he sat down at his dad's computer and taught himself to use the sophisticated graphics program. Does it make sense that John started a computer typesetting business when he was in high school? Yes. In college John came up with the idea for a graphic arts company and started it while still a student. Today—after a three-year sojourn in Hollywood, where he picked up a lot of helpful computer and graphic art skills—he's back building his college business, designing logos, creating decals, and selling them to college bookstores across the country.

Allow children to be happy in their own way, for what better way will they ever find?
                                        —Samuel Johnson

Sure, we're tempted to suggest that he work for a larger company for a while, learn what he can there, and enjoy its resources and benefits—health and dental insurance are nice things to have. But he's following the dream within him, and we're trying to support that. It's actually fun while driving down the road to spot a college insignia that he designed and manufactured on the back windshield of a car.

BALANCING DREAMS WITH REALITY

Perhaps you're wondering what to do if a child's dream seems truly unrealistic. I recently met a woman with this problem, and she handled it in a very wise way. Liz told me that her daughter announced one night at dinner her plan to drop out of college after only one semester and become a jewelry designer. She planned to move to New York, halfway across the country, where she'd quickly grow famous and rich and maybe even become the next David Yurman.

An unfulfilled vocation drains the color from a man's entire existence.

—Honoré de Balzac

The mother's response was twofold: First, she didn't squelch the dream. Instead, she encouraged her daughter to envision what types of things she would need to know to become a successful jewelry designer. They brainstormed a bit and agreed it would be helpful to have some business and accounting knowledge. Perhaps understanding world economics would help; this would assist her when she was buying raw materials. Strategies for sales and marketing would be important, and some art classes would hone her skills. Together they decided that a business major would be a good background for her future success and that she could take some art classes as electives. Liz said her daughter went back to college the next semester with new zeal.

That's what I call a savvy mom: encouraging her daughter's dreams while at the same time helping her keep her feet planted on the ground of reality. Isn't this what we all really want to do for our children? Not only did she avoid pouring cold water on her daughter's passion, she helped her daughter sharpen a vision that will ensure more energy as she tackles her schoolwork. When she's sitting in accounting class—probably not a course a jewelry designer would choose—she can keep the end goal in sight.

What about you? Have you been a dreambuilder or a dreambuster? It's never too late to become a dreambuilder in a child's life. Here are some things you can do to help your young adult discover his destiny.

1. Brainstorm with your child and make a list of things he has enjoyed doing over the years. Look for the common elements: Was he alone or working with a team? Did he enjoy performing at something or working behind the scenes? Did he work on the project until the end or get bored midstream? Then think of possible careers in which he would use those skills.

We are either progressing or retrograding all the while; there is no such thing as remaining stationary in life.

—James Freeman Clarke

For example, your daughter might list that she enjoyed being chosen to create the bulletin boards for her classrooms in the third and fourth grades. She volunteered to make posters for the antilitter campaign in seventh grade and created the student government flyers in ninth grade. She didn't like distributing the flyers, though. In high school she headed the drama production team in charge of creating the backdrop. She enjoyed most of her responsibilities there except for dealing with students who didn't meet their deadlines or show up at meetings. Instead of confronting them, she decided it was easier just to do it herself.

One can study her list and see that all the things she enjoyed involved using her artistic skills. She liked working by herself more than working with a team, and she didn't like managing people. Some careers she might want to consider are graphic design, advertising, and set design for theater.

My business is not to remake myself, but make the absolute best of what God made.

—Robert Browning

---

2. Help your child think through his dreams. He should ask himself:

- Why do I want to do this?

- What steps do I need to take to be ready if an opportunity to fulfill my dream comes about?

- If I could make a difference in the world, what would I do?

- How would other people benefit if my dream came true?

- What is most important to me in life? How will I maintain my priorities if my dream comes true?

- Is this a good time for my dream to come to pass?

- Would I be able to use my gifts and talents if I pursued this dream?

- Would the dream bring out the best in me?

- Does my dream have confirmation from others? (Has anyone said, "Hey, John, I think you'd make a really good attorney"?)

- Is this dream one that I should pursue myself, or do I need others to help me make it happen?

- What do I see myself doing on a daily basis?

- Is there something I should do today to move toward this dream?

3. Listen carefully to what your child tells you about her dreams. Even if you think they are outlandish, don't react. Listen. Try to get behind the words to the deep longings of what your child really wants.

Optimism is the faith that leads to achievement. Nothing can be done without hope.

—Helen Keller

---

4. Encourage your young adult to seek out a summer job that would allow him to explore some of the careers in which he's interested. Many companies offer summer internships. They don't pay well—some don't pay at all—but they're priceless in terms of learning and focusing on future careers.

5. Offer to help your student's high school start a career day program in which students spend a half day off campus "shadowing" someone whose job interests them. The visits should be set up and approved before the career day. Suggest that students write a summary of the visit: the occupation they observed,

the name and title of the person they shadowed, the degree or specialized training needed for the position, an overview of their visit, what they liked most and least about the job, and an approximate entry-level salary.

If a man is called to be a street sweeper, he should sweep streets even as Michelangelo painted, or Beethoven composed music, or Shakespeare wrote poetry. He should sweep streets so well that all the hosts of heaven and earth will pause to say, "Here lived a great street sweeper who did his job well."

—Martin Luther King, Jr.

---

6. Consider paying for your child to take an aptitude or gift-assessment test. Most college students now change majors at least twice, requiring one or more extra years of college. This costs parents thousands of extra dollars. A test can help pinpoint your child's skills and talents and may help her identify what would be wise—and not so wise—career choices. There are many good tests out there, in a wide price range. We used The Giftedness Center in Dallas, Texas (www.TheGiftednessCenter.com), and were very pleased. They helped our boys (and us, as well) identify inborn core strengths and natural motivation which helps them make meaningful choices for their life and work.

7. Suggest that your child read books that will help focus her career goals. We found the following very helpful:

The Power of Uniqueness by Arthur F. Miller, Jr., and William Hendricks (Zondervan, 2002)

The On-Purpose Person: Making Your Life Make Sense by Kevin W. McCarthy (Piñon Press, 1992)

Inc. Your Dreams: For Any Woman Who Is Thinking about Her Own Business by Rebecca Maddox (Viking, 1995)

What Color Is Your Parachute? by Richard Bolles (Ten Speed Press, 2000)

The Path: Creating Your Mission Statement for Work and for Life by Laurie Beth Jones (Hyperion, 1996)

Finding a Job You Can Love by Ralph Mattson and Arthur Miller (Thomas Nelson, 1982)

The Call: Finding and Fulfilling the Central Purpose of Your Life by Os Guinness (Word Publishing, 1998)

Always be a first-rate version of yourself, instead of a second rate version of somebody else.
                                        —Judy Garland

---

8. If your child is living at home, don't allow her to sit around watching TV, waiting for the right job to find her. If she's able to work, she needs to get a job and do what she can until she can do what she loves.

9. Be aware that some young adults need extra help. They may take more time than other kids their age to pursue a specific goal; it may help if you guide them in developing a time line or a budget to get something accomplished. Note: If your child seems down a lot and has no desire to do anything, he may

be struggling with clinical depression, something that requires treatment through medication and/or counseling. Seek professional help through your primary-care physician.

GETTING READY FOR YOUR DREAM TO COME TRUE

Recently, a twenty-nine-year-old woman asked me for advice. She loved her career as a kindergarten teacher but dreamed of being a wife and mother. She didn't want to be single anymore. I asked how she was preparing for the role she longed to fulfill, and she had no idea what I was talking about.

Unfortunately, fairy godmothers exist only in the movies. No dream—no matter what size—will come to fruition on its own. It takes hard work to make it happen. I told the young woman it was important to put herself in the right position physically and mentally so that she'd be ready if and when Mr. Right was. She needed to make spiritual growth a priority so that her spirit would be sensitive about whether a certain man was the right one for her.

Don't wait for your ship to come in; swim out to it.
—Anonymous

We also discussed being mentally prepared for marriage: learning healthy communication techniques, thinking through the implications for her life and schedule. We talked about becoming physically prepared: getting in shape, building healthy habits that would last a lifetime. And we talked about getting emotionally prepared: becoming comfortable with who she was and learning healthy ways to deal with anger, depression, stress.

She agreed that she could be a lot busier in the pursuit of her dream. Then I suggested one more thing: She should "play in traffic." She wouldn't get "hit" sitting at home, hoping Mr. Right would show up on her doorstep. That thinking is tantamount to wishing a million dollars would show up in your bank account. She needed to get out and meet new people, get involved in community affairs and at her church, work out at a gym, join professional associations, in short, put herself in the right place to meet Mr. Right.

The secret in life is for a man to be ready for his opportunity when it comes.

—Benjamin Disraeli

If this story has a familiar ring, no matter what career your adult child is dreaming of, consider taking her out to dinner and discussing the following questions in a loving, affirming way. Talk about the fact that whatever our dreams are, we need to be prepared.

- What do you do in your spare time? How can you be prepared for the career of your dreams?

- Have you

    ○ Been to a trade show or convention on the topic of your dream?

    ○ Bought any new books or tapes pertaining to your dream?

    ○ Gone out of your way to look for something that has to do with your dream?

    ○ Started a journal and recorded the steps you are taking toward your dream?

- Told anyone else about your dream?

- Prayed about your dream? How much?

- Gone on a spiritual retreat to be quiet and listen to what's going on in your heart and soul?

HOW TO HELP YOUR ADULT CHILDREN ENVISION WHAT THEY COULD BE

It's not unusual for a young adult just out of college or the military not to know what he wants to do. Perhaps a daughter majored in elementary education only to learn during her student-teaching senior year that she really didn't like to teach. Or maybe a son joined the military to see the world, and now all he knows is that he wants a job that doesn't require travel. There are thirty-, forty-, and fifty-year-olds who don't know what to do with the rest of their lives either.

The way to get ahead is to start now. If you start now, you will know a lot next year that you don't know now and that you would not have known next year if you had waited.

—William Feather

It's all too easy to get discouraged when we don't have a direction in life. At those times we tend to focus on what we're not doing or what doors are not open to us. But when that happens, we are not seeing the whole picture, and despair can set in. That's not healthy or helpful.

To help your adult child avoid—or begin digging out of—such frustration, help her take some proactive steps toward discovering a dream into which she can pour her energies. Guide her to do the following:

- Do a rigorous, honest evaluation of both her strong points and her limitations. Make sure she gives herself credit where it's due; when one is discouraged, one usually sees oneself in negative terms.

- View her accomplishments in the best light. Maybe she's finished only thirty hours toward a nursing degree. That's thirty more than none!

- Encourage her to explore the areas that have always interested her. She needn't narrow her search for a dream within a week or a month, but she should begin—and keep—looking till something grabs her attention and won't let go.

Progress is looking forward intelligently, looking within critically, and moving on incessantly.

—Waldo Pondray Warren

- Suggest she ask adults she trusts—perhaps previous employers—for feedback: At what has she shown special skill? Does she seem particularly talented in certain areas—with people, animals, machines? Where has she been successful so far in her life?

WHAT HE'S GOT GOING FOR HIM

Consider the following categories when reminding your child of his or her assets. Schedule some time to sit down together and make a list:

Personal strengths: What are you good at? What do you love to do?

Learned skills: What skills have you gained, formally or informally, over the course of your life?

Education: What knowledge have you acquired formally?

Experiences: What perspectives or insights have you picked up along the way?

Family, friends, and their network: You are probably only one or two persons away from knowing someone who has what you need or knows what you need to know.

Access to authority and expertise: Who do you know who can open doors for you and give you the information you need?

Special environmental opportunities: What freedoms and resources do you have available to you in your city, state, or country?

Physical abilities and attributes: What physical traits do you have going for you?

Financial resources: To what financial assets do you have access?

Equally important is identifying what they don't want, or like, to do. Ask your son or daughter questions like these as well.

- Do you like working with a team or independently on projects?

- Are you a "big picture" person, or do you enjoy making sure the details are taken care of?

- Does it help you to have a structured environment—a certain time to arrive and leave work, standard operating procedures in place—or are you self-disciplined enough get work done at your own pace in an unstructured environment?

Restlessness and discontent are the necessities of progress.
                                        —Thomas Alva Edison

- Do you like deadlines?
- Do you like to travel?

SIFTING FOR SPECIFICS

As your adult child tries to sift his desires and dreams, help him think about them in very practical terms. Tell him to imagine himself in his dream situation. For example, say he envisions a dream job. What does the office look like? What tasks would he spend the most time on? What kind of people would he like to work with?

If he has trouble painting even a general picture, suggest the following exercises. He needn't limit himself to three answers for each question, but I've found that the first three things that come immediately to one's mind often are one's heart's secret desires.

- Write down three things you have enjoyed doing and would like to do more. Sewing? Working math equations? Helping people solve problems? Reading? Taking classes? Jogging? Cooking?

- Write down three things you would like to try at least once to see if you like them. Volunteering at a food bank? Windsurfing? Writing and submitting an article to the local newspaper?

- Write down three things you'd like to change about your appearance.

- Write down three habits you'd like to lose.

- Write down three habits you'd like to incorporate into your life.

- Write down three hobbies that sound like fun.

- Write down three skills you would like to learn.

- Find a bulletin for a local community college. Write down three classes that sound interesting.

- Look at the want ads in the newspaper and note three jobs that sound interesting.

Work is the natural exercise and function of man. . . . Work is not primarily a thing one does to live, but the thing one lives to do. It is, or should be, the full expression of the worker's faculties, the thing in which he finds spiritual, mental, and bodily satisfaction, the medium in which he offers himself to God.

—Dorothy Sayers

Answering these questions will draw him closer to targeting the future of his dreams.

STEP BY STEP AND DAY BY DAY

When our adult children lack direction, they shouldn't use that as an excuse to do nothing. Just as the single woman discovered many actions she could take to prepare herself for her specific dream, any young adult can take steps to improve himself in general ways. These improvements will help him grow mentally, physically, spiritually, emotionally, and socially; in short, they'll serve him well no matter what he ends up doing.

The fact is, inertia breeds itself; so does action.

Sample Evaluation/Envision Exercise

To get started, your young adult can take stock of his or her overall lifestyle. Here's what a sample review might look like. It involves taking stock of what is and looking at what could be.

Physical Assessment What do I look like now? What do I want to look like? What could be better? How could I could be healthier? More balanced? More attractive?

- Schedule a physical examination. (Short-term: Do this ASAP.)

- Go through wardrobe and give away clothes I don't wear anymore. (Short-term.)

- Buy new clothes. (Long-term. See below.)

- Talk with my hairdresser or barber about an easier, updated style. (Short-term.)

- I've been feeling run-down lately. Get more exercise and sleep. (Short-term: Add a ten-minute walk to my day. Long-term: Build up to a more rigorous exercise program. Join a gym. After six months, reevaluate sleep needs in light of exercise.)

- Look into weight-loss programs. (Wait until I lose weight to buy clothes? Research options ASAP.)

- My fingernails need help. (Schedule and budget for monthly manicures.)

- Look into new cosmetics product line. (Want something that's simple to use but will help my dry skin.)

Emotional Assessment. What do I feel like now? What do I want to feel like? What could be better? How could I be emotionally healthier?

- Work on my attitude. (Short-term: ASAP. Remind myself what I have to be grateful for.)

- Get more exercise and sleep. (See above.)

- Spend more time with people who encourage me.

- Find quotes that remind me that when life hands me lemons, I can make lemonade or a soufflé. Post them where I'll see them.

- Schedule fun time for myself. (Short-term: Call a friend and ask her out for lunch. Long-term: Look ahead at my calendar and make sure I'm scheduling fun activities as well as work-related things.)

- Begin to deal with ongoing problems; don't assume they'll go away by themselves, and don't try to bury feelings of sadness or frustration. (Short-term: Make some notes about my emotional life and how I'd like it to change. Long-term: Explore whether I might want to enlist the help of a professional counselor.)

- Have a plan for blah days. (Short-term: Make a list of pick-me-ups I can pull off in a pinch, such as taking in a matinee, getting a massage, or working on a favorite but neglected hobby.)

Mental Assessment How knowledgeable am I now? How knowledgeable do I want to be? How could I make myself more interesting?

- Start a list of books I want to read this year. (Renew library card. Budget for books I want to buy.)

- Look into a computer class. (Call a college. Call computer manufacturers to see what they recommend.)

- Read the daily newspaper beyond the comics and entertainment sections.

- Make a work space for reading and writing at home.

- Start a book group. (Long-term: Get a group going. Short-term: Invite two friends to read a book and meet to discuss it.)

- Sign up for lecture series. (Check different options at library and college. Invite a friend to join me?)

Spiritual Assessment How well do I react to daily ups and downs? How could I be healthier? More balanced? More serene?

- Set aside quiet time for prayer every day. (Begin now. Continue. Write it in my schedule.)

- Take a class at church. (Long-term: Look into fall offerings.)

- Make a list of books in this area I want to read. (Combine with other book list above.)

- Take a bigger chunk of time out to grow spiritually. (Long-term: Look into going away on a spiritual retreat.)

- Share my spiritual life with others. (Ongoing. Schedule time with my friends or pastor to talk about concerns we have for our spiritual lives. Maybe take a retreat together. See above.)

- Remind myself that God provides. (Short-term: Find inspirational quotes so that I remember that this is

true. Write them out and place them where I'll see
them frequently.)

• Seek out a spiritual mentor. (Pastor? Wise friend?
Find someone who can recommend books to read
and talk with me.)

When our children were younger, they saw life with
courage and excitement: "I want to be a Supreme Court jus-
tice." "I want to race horses." "I will study volcanoes." As reality and age whittled their dreams, they sometimes aimed lower
("I'd like to study law") and sometimes envisioned new voca-
tions altogether ("I want to teach kindergarten"). The shape
shifting dreams take is normal and natural. All that is important is that your child, and you as her guide, take into account
the ways she's made and gifted and let those characteristics
form the dreams she actually pursues. Your role here is
immensely important: You will cheer her on her way, or you
will deflate her for years to come. Choose wisely—your children and mine will create the future.

5

Leave the Porch Light On and the Home Fire Burning

Home is the place where, when you have to go there they have to take you in.
—Robert Frost

When I can no longer bear to think of the victims of broken homes, I begin to think of the victims of intact ones.
—Peter De Vries

A couple of years ago I attended the wedding of an old friend's daughter. Six months later I ran into Ellen at the mall and asked if the newlyweds were coming home for the holidays. She told me in a huff that her daughter had called (she and her new husband lived out of state) to say that they were coming home for Christmas but were going to "camp out" at her husband's parents' home. Ellen was incensed and hurt, but quite frankly, I wasn't all that surprised. I remembered when her daughter was in high school. The kids didn't want to hang out at her house then either. Ellen was always nagging them about their music being too loud or their leaving crumbs on the countertops.

Ellen's story is a wake-up call for all of us. If our kids aren't coming home as much as we'd like, is it possible that our porch light has gone out—that our kids feel they're not welcome or would rather be elsewhere?

I love to go back home! I love the smell when I walk through the door, I love sleeping in my old bed, seeing my dog, and catching up on life with my parents. I usually can't stay very long because of my job, but going home always makes me feel better than before I arrived.

—Amy, age 27

MAKING YOUR HOME A MAGNET

"Oh, the fun of arriving at a house and feeling the spark that tells you that you are going to have a good time." Author Mark Hampton hit the nail on the head for me. This is the end goal of the details and fuss I go to before my kids come home. I want it to be a magnet that draws them effortlessly back. Many places vie for my kids' time and attention; I want my home to be a strong pull.

Ah! There's nothing like staying home for real comfort.
—Jane Austen

Have you ever stopped to think about what makes home a place everyone wants to be? Whether it's a castle or a cottage, a condo or a penthouse, a cabin or a studio, every home has certain ingredients that make it appealing over every other home in the world. While beautiful appointments and classically styled furniture are nice, they don't necessarily exude comfort—the key to making home homey.

Maybe when your kids were living at home, your house became like a fast-food drivethrough, where family members rushed in, grabbed a bite to eat and a clean shirt, asked for money, exchanged a few words, and then rushed out again. On the other hand, perhaps it was an empty shell; people came there to sleep, but never to congregate. Maybe the emptiness rattled and disappointed you.

What kind of home do you want to have? What do you hope will happen there: Extended family get-togethers? Sunday dinners? Baby showers? Family reunions? Holiday celebrations? Rollicking weekends with the grandchildren? It's never too late to do home improvement. Regardless of whether your child is married, single, with or without children, there are some simple things you can do to help assure that your home is on everyone's list of drop-in or vacation destinations. Here are some ways to magnetize your home.

1. *Welcome your kids with open arms.*

   - Make sure they know their coming home is not a hassle. Try to prepare as much as possible before they come so you won't be running around, stressed out, when they arrive.

   - Start on a positive note. Compliment your son- or daughter-in-law on clothing, hairstyle, timeliness of arrival—anything. Let your family know right away that you're happy to see them.

   - Turn off the television and turn on your answering machine when they arrive.

When there's room in the heart there's room in the house.
                                    —Danish proverb

---

2. *Make your house as comfy and cozy as possible.* Ask yourself some questions: Is the entry inviting? What do you smell when you walk through the door? Is the kitchen sending out wonderful aromas? Are there

places to hang coats and hats, then comfy places to plop after a long day? Are the bathrooms clean? Is the house reasonably neat—not spotless, just tidy?

If you live in the same house where your child grew up, discuss how he or she would like to store things left behind. That way the old room will be appealing but not cluttered, and you can outfit it for his or her own family. Consider these elements when updating:

- Does the room need new curtains or lampshades?

- Is the mattress comfortable? Sleep on it yourself to see.

- Pillows: it's nice to have one firm one, a soft one, a nonallergenic one, and one for a person to prop himself up on to read.

- Set up a special place for mail they continue to get at your house.

- Provide interesting books, magazines, and catalogs.

- Make sure windows have shades or curtains that can be pulled for privacy and to shut out light.

- Provide a bedside reading lamp with three-way bulb.

- Supply the nightstand with radio, alarm clock, tissues, and wastebasket.

- Put disposable cups in the bathroom, or a bottle of water.

- Hang a mirror, preferably full length but at least from waist up.

- Supply a flashlight for unexpected power outages.

- Make sure the closet is amply cleared for a family's belongings, including their suitcases. Offer sturdy hangers.

- Clear out a dresser drawer or two if possible.

- Place a small vase of fresh flowers or a small plant on the dresser or nightstand.

- Invest in a couple of large terrycloth bathrobes in case guests don't bring any.

- Put an extra hair dryer in the bathroom, as well as sample sizes of toothpaste and shampoo. Install a nightlight.

- Make sure guests know where they can adjust the temperature in their room.

- Make sure your kids can touch base with the office, check e-mails—feel connected to the "outside world." Offer use of your computer and phone.

3. *Provide good food for the body.*

- Plan ahead for any food allergies or dietary restrictions.

- When your son- or daughter-in-law visits for the first time, show him or her around the kitchen. Explain how the coffeemaker works and show where the supplies are.

- For easy access, place breakfast foods and drinks on counter in the morning. Let everyone serve him- or herself.

- Discuss a dinner schedule that works for everyone. Plan to serve some of your child's old favorites.

4. *Provide nourishment for the mind and spirit.*

   - Keep books and current magazines available for grown-ups and kids alike.

   - Keep hobby supplies handy so your kids can tackle projects in free moments.

   - Have some board games, playing cards, jigsaw puzzles on hand

   - Keep the tone and conversation as upbeat as possible.

   - Curb complaining and talk about the good in your life.

   - Teach your grandkids by example to enjoy life deeply—to keep problems in their places and celebrate living in spite of them.

   - Start conversations with pleasant inquiries, not self-centered venting

   - Let people know you care on a deep level about them.

   - Let your kids feel your affection every time they enter the house.

5. *Make your house kid-friendly.* Here's one mom's story of how she learned a big lesson about this. I met Patricia at a bookstore where I had presented a seminar. She complained to me that her son and daughter-in-law never wanted to come over to her house. (They all live in the same city.) They spend a lot of

time with the daughter-in-law's parents, which makes the woman sad because she and her husband would like to see the grandchildren more.

As we continued to talk, I began asking Patricia questions about her home. As she described it, I realized it was an "adult" house. She had lots of antiques, no toys, and she made clear that she doesn't like messes. In short, her house was an uncomfortable place for kids.

I told her she had to make a choice: Did she want a perfectly appointed, spic-and-span home, or did she want a place her son's family raved to visit?

We talked about this and she saw the need to make her home more family-friendly. She wrote to me a few months later and told me things were much better—the kids and grandkids were coming over more. The steps she took are noteworthy:

- She had a heart-to-heart talk with her son and daughter-in-law and asked them specifically what would make her home attractive for visits.

- She designated a lower cupboard in the kitchen for the grandkids and bought them some plastic dishes.

- She cleaned out a closet and made it the kids'— she stocked it with toys, games, and dress-up clothes.

- She started a collection of children's DVDs, CDs, and books.

- She bought some play equipment for the backyard.

- She stopped compulsively cleaning up after everyone.

- She kept everyone's favorites drinks and snacks on hand.

Some other suggestions:

- Decide how much baby gear you can provide. Parents will be thrilled not to have to pack high chairs, strollers, playpens, and so on. Consider stocking up on disposable diapers, bibs, and a few jars of baby food.

- Let parents know they're welcome to use the washer and dryer at any time. Kids get soiled easily, so parents will need to do laundry at some point. (Also see "Grandchildproof Your Home," page 168)

A home is no home unless it contains food and fire for the mind as well as for the body.

—Margaret Fuller

WHAT MAKES A HOME ATTRACT OR REPEL

I asked college students and young adults in the marketplace why they did or did not enjoy going back home. Their answers may surprise you—and inspire you to make changes. Here's what I heard:

I like to go back home because

- I miss my mom's cooking.

- I like to watch sports on TV with my dad.

- I get to spend time with my sister, and I get to see my dogs.

- I can relax and forget about the stress of school.

- I know my parents love me unconditionally.
- I don't have to do everything for myself. I never knew how much my mom worked, doing the grocery shopping, laundry, and house cleaning. Now that I'm on my own, I appreciate what she did.
- I just like being with my parents.
- I get to attend my old church.
- I like sleeping in my bed.
- I like the smell of our house when I walk in the door.
- My dad takes me to my favorite restaurant.
- I can talk to my parents about issues in my life. They're really good about listening and giving me wise advice. They don't lecture or pressure me.
- I like sitting around the dinner table with my family and talking about what's going on in our lives.
- My parents are interested in my life. They encourage me a lot.
- My parents pamper me when I go home. It's like a vacation. I work twelve-hour days, and so I *need* a vacation!

I don't like to go home because

- My parents fight.
- My parents nag me a lot.

- My mother's always down because of my rebellious little sister. I think she should at least be happy that I turned out okay.

- My mother never wants me to leave. I wish she'd get a life of her own.

- When I go home, I'm usually tired. My parents want me to do chores just like I did when I lived at home.

- My parents pry into my love life. They're so worried I won't get married.

- My parents complain about everything. I don't call enough, they don't like whom I'm dating, they don't like what I'm planning to do when I graduate.

- No one's ever there. My parents are busy with their own lives. But that's the way it's always been.

- It doesn't feel like home. My parents moved right after I left home.

- I have to split my time between my mom's house and my dad's apartment. It's easier not to go at all.

- My faith has become very important to me. My parents are not supportive of my spiritual choices.

- My mother criticizes the way we're raising our kids.

- I can't do anything right. I'm tired of hearing that.

YOUNG MARRIEDS TALK ABOUT
GOING HOME

My wife and I are leaving next week for our obliga-
tory twice-a-year visit to my parents' home. I feel
guilty that we don't go more than that, but the truth
is, I don't want to. The minute I walk in the door
my dad has a project for me to work on: sod the
yard, fix the roof, help him put new brakes on his
car. I don't mind helping him with projects; I used
to when I lived at home. But now I just feel like a
hired hand. I hear my friends talk about how they
go back to visit their parents and play golf with their
dads and their moms fix their favorite meal. I would
like that.

—Andrew, age 30

I wish my parents (my child's grandparents) would
understand how hard it is for us to visit them when
their house is full of expensive decor and light-col-
ored carpets and upholstery. Of course they want
us to come and visit, but we're on pins and needles
the whole time we're there, afraid our toddler is
going to break or soil something. I think parents
who are new to this empty-nest, first-time-grand-
parents thing should think long and hard: Do they
want to have a house that looks like a photo in
Architectural Digest, or do they want a comfortable
home that welcomes kids and grandkids? They
considered that when we were growing up. Mom
always chose fabrics and flooring that didn't show
dirt. My friends and I liked hanging out there and

she liked having us there. I don't know why she thinks it's different now.

—Cindy, age 35

HOME AGAIN

Having grown-up children return to the nest is becoming more and more common. In May 2002, *USA Today* reported that 60 percent of graduating college students would move back home to live with their parents. Some people call this the boomerang syndrome, implying the negative notion that parents have tried tossing their children out into the world only to have them return again and again.

Yet the fact that more young adults are living at home with their parents is not necessarily a bad thing; in fact, extended time together can be a surprisingly enriching experience. It's just that many of us didn't have this in our plans. Many parents anticipate that once their kids move out, they will have a perpetually clean house, a breezy schedule, and a phone that rarely rings. When grown kids move back home, we may have at best mixed emotions and at worst depression and frustration.

The thing about having a baby is that thereafter you have it.

—Jean Kerr

There are a number of reasons why adult kids come back home. Some simply don't know how to live on their own. If they were indulged and showered with attention while growing up, never having to do much for themselves, they may need further education on the basics of how to run their homes and lives. At the other end of the spectrum are kids who for whatever reason didn't get enough attention. Seeking the love and acceptance they crave, these grown children continue to vie for—and even demand—their parents' attention. This is a recipe for resentment. Parents who find themselves in this situation often feel less than gracious about sharing their home, time, and resources, and this results in their children being even more desperate to feel loved.

A large number of young adults move back home as part of a temporary plan to save money, pay school debts, cut costs while getting a degree, or build a nest egg for the future. Maybe they see it as a good place to stay while looking for a job or waiting to get married. If they don't start a career in their area of expertise, they usually are working someplace, and many are contributing to household expenses.

It sometimes happens, even in the best of families, that a baby is born. This is not necessarily cause for alarm. The important thing is to keep your wits about you and borrow some money.

—Elinor Goulding Smith

Regardless of how we, the parents, feel about this midlife turn of events, we can make the back-to-the-nest-again experience work well for the whole family. Sure, there will be some tension, but as in all relationships, a little work and a positive attitude go a long way. Our efforts to make our home a warm, welcoming place where all family members can grow toward their full potential will pay huge dividends. But it's important to remind ourselves that when our young adult moves back home, we're still parenting, although we're doing it in different ways.

PARENTING: ACT II

It was a pleasant surprise when at the age of twenty-seven our oldest son asked to move home from another state for a few months while he worked on saving money and growing a business he had started in college. We really liked having him home: He was helpful with household chores and respectful of our time and space, plus I loved having in-house tech support. It was an all-around good experience for our family.

After I made a comment at a speaking engagement about our son moving back home, a woman I'll call Susan introduced herself and told me that her experience with her daughter Elizabeth had been equally satisfying. Elizabeth moved home for the summer after college graduation and before starting law school. Susan said they made lots of great memories and thoroughly enjoyed each other.

Every parent is at some time the father of the unreturned prodigal, with nothing to do but keep his house open to hope.

—John Anthony Ciardi

But Susan's other daughter was a different story. Allison, six years younger than Elizabeth, moved back home from necessity. She was out of money and out of ideas about a career or life plan. Much to her parents' dismay, Allison's college career had been dotted with poor grades and run-ins with the dean. When she finally managed to graduate, she couldn't figure out what she wanted to do, and so she traveled in Europe for a semester, with Mom and Dad footing the bill. Then, in an effort to figure out life, she came back to the States and moved in with her parents, who were by that time accustomed to an empty nest.

It wasn't easy to have Allison back home. With the advent of her free schedule, Susan had decided to go back to college to get certified as a family therapist; she had grown accustomed to quiet study time at home. Once settled in, Allison was anxious to get back to the soap operas she had followed faithfully in high school and college. When her mom asked her to turn them off, Allison would roll her eyes and comply. (They'd fought this battle before, when she was in high school.) But every day Allison would turn the soaps back on, and she and Susan would go through the same routine—although Susan's ire was growing stronger by the week.

There are times when parenthood seems like nothing but feeding the mouth that bites you.
—Peter De Vries

Eventually, every day turned into a shouting match—not what Susan had meant to happen. During the course of her studies, though, Susan began reading about older kids who struggle to grow up. They simply aren't ready to face the responsibilities of independence quite yet. If parents understand this and are patient, these kids eventually can mature, move out on their own, and lead productive and meaningful lives. They just need some additional attention and guidance to do this.

Children need love, especially when they don't deserve it.
—Harold S. Hulbert

Susan realized that her daughter needed more growing-up time and that she, the mother, had some things to learn as well. In fact, as the months passed and Susan lovingly enforced a few house rules, boundaries, and the need to get a job, she did learn a few things, namely, how Allison felt about following in the shadow of a "perfect" older sister. Susan realized that Allison needed some extra doses of love, support, and affection. Over time she became thankful for this unexpected experience of having Allison at home because she was able to rectify her past mistake of showcasing Elizabeth. And all her effort paid off: Over the months Allison blossomed into a lovely, purposeful young lady.

MAKING HOMECOMING A HAPPY EXPERIENCE

No matter what reason your child had for coming home to live, there are actions you can take to make this a more pleasant experience for everyone. Working together to establish a living arrangement with loving but firm guidelines is critical. When adult children move back home, you don't have to give up your house, pocketbook, and schedule to support them. But it does mean you may need to give a generous amount of love, guidance, sympathy, and creative energy to help them get out of the nest and be able to support themselves. Here are ten suggestions to help you get off to a good start with your own home-again experience.

1. *Schedule a family meeting.* Soon after your child moves back, have a family meeting. Fix a favorite snack or dessert; good food has a way of fostering goodwill and cooperation. Use this time first of all to affirm your love and make sure your child knows you're glad to have him home. Talk about how you want this extended visit back home to be a good one for him and for you and state that you want your home to be a positive place for all of you.

2. *Set a deadline.* Establish a time limit for the renesting experience. This date can be flexible; maybe you agree it will be a two-month experience but realize after two months that you need to push the move-out day back another month or two. That's fine, but you should establish some sense of how long the arrangement will last up-front. All family members will feel more relaxed if they know there is a time limit.

3. *Establish some goals and a way to evaluate progress.* If your adult child comes back home with the goal of accomplishing something, such as finding a job, finishing a degree, or dealing with an addiction, talk about how you look forward to seeing some progress. You know your child's ability to be self-directed. Some young adults will discipline themselves to meet their goals; other will need accountability. You may need to set a time weekly to discuss the job search, meet with the child's therapist or AA sponsor, or look over school assignments and grades together.

Our chief want in life is somebody who will make us do what we can.

—Ralph Waldo Emerson

---

4. *Set some financial parameters.* Formulate a financial agreement that will take into account the monetary goals and situations of all family members. Schedule a time at least twice a month for bill paying. Make sure everyone knows what the expenses are and each person's appropriate contribution. In the rare event that a young person cannot make any financial con-

tribution to the household, she can make other con-
tributions, such as cleaning, doing yard work or
repairs, running errands—anything that will aid the
other family members.

5. *Divide up chores and household responsibilities.*
   Anyone who has the privilege of living under the
   roof of a home should help with the upkeep and
   running of that home. Divvy up household chores—
   cooking, cleaning, grocery shopping, taking out the
   garbage—between family members. Let everyone be
   in charge of his or her own laundry.

6. *Establish some basic rules of common courtesy.* Discuss
   what you consider civil behavior and emphasize the
   need to treat one another politely. If your family
   didn't practice this in your home when your child
   was younger, be careful that you don't approach
   making a change in a confrontational manner. Don't
   say, "Things are going to be different around here!"
   Instead, broach the subject calmly, as you would
   with any other adult. That's really the message you
   want to send to your child: "Now that you are an
   adult, I expect you, as I do myself, to behave as an
   adult." It's likely that you and your grown child share
   the same desire anyway: to be treated in a respectful
   manner.

LIFE IS NOT ALWAYS EASY

A fifty-one-year-old father shared his story with me.
"When my wife and I divorced, it was very hard on
our kids. They all reacted in different ways, but our
youngest daughter sought consolation in a group of

kids who accepted her . . . and introduced her to drugs. She became a heroin addict, and at age twenty-one she was pregnant by another heroin addict. She came to me, needing help: She wanted to keep her baby and to get her life back on track.

"I helped her move her things into my house and get into a drug rehab program. From the start I told her that she was a grown-up now—an adult moving into another adult's home—and I would treat her that way. I expected her to give me the same respect I gave her. That was eighteen months ago.

"Now she is drug-free and thankfully has a healthy, beautiful baby. I told her I would pay for her college education now just as I would have when she was eighteen; I considered this merely a late start. She and the baby moved out into an apartment, and she found a good neighborhood Mother's Day Out program to help while she was in school.

"If you had told me this is what my life would be like in my early fifties, I wouldn't have believed it and wouldn't have wished it on myself either. But this difficult experience has been one of the most wonderful of my life. I made some sacrifices, but I believe that putting some of my personal desires on the back burner for a while so that I could help my daughter get back on her feet has made me feel better about my life than I would have if I had only been doing my own things. I guess that's what parenting is about."

7. *Discuss privacy.* Talk about the importance of privacy and try to come up with a plan that will give everyone under your roof some personal space and time.

You also may need to discuss everyone's requests to use separate parts of the house for meetings or entertaining and how you can accommodate each other.

A key to healthy family relationships is reciprocal respect. This means we acknowledge and heed each other's boundaries—wherever we live.

—Bill Peel

---

8. *Set some specific boundaries.* Another area you'll need to address with "new" people living in the house is boundaries, and boundary invasion often needs to be spelled out. Sometimes kids (and parents, too) know they're crossing the line; other times they're totally unaware of it. Either way, the result is the same: strained relationships, awkward conversations, and frequent feelings of irritation.

You can avoid this friction by talking together about what the following guidelines for avoiding boundary invasion mean in your family:

- Accepting a person's refusal if you ask for time and/or assistance.

- Not abusing someone's kindness by requiring far more time and attention than you suggested you would need.

- Returning items you borrowed in their original condition and on time. Replace anything you break or lose.

- Getting a person's approval for the use of his belongings or personal property.

- Concluding the conversation when the person has said she is busy or must leave.

- Consulting a person before offering his help or making promises for him.

- Waiting for an invitation to invade someone's space, explore her property, go through her purse or backpack, or peruse closed doors and cupboards.

- Accepting a person's choice to keep some information private.

- Not violating a person's integrity by persistently asking him to go against his better judgment.

- Keeping engagements and appointments on time. Calling if we're running late.

9. *Give yourself permission to seek outside help.* Big changes in life are sometimes more than we can handle alone, and an adult child moving back home can be a big change. Sometimes we need the help of experts. Few of us hesitate to see a physician when we're ill. In my opinion, asking a counselor for help through a personal emotional crisis, seeking the guidance of a spiritual adviser in a crisis of faith, or meeting with a qualified family therapist when an issue has the potential of tearing a family apart is well worth every penny and all the time investment it requires. Talking with a counselor can provide new insights into handling conflicts within our families and healing the pain of the past. An objective outsider also can help you know how and when it's time to nudge an overly dependent child out into the world on his or her own.

10. *Regularly remind each other of your love.* Declare and show each other your love in some way every day. Sign your notes "Love, Mom"; end phone conversations with "I love you."

My parents constantly tell me how proud they are of me. I certainly wasn't a perfect child: I went through some rebellious years that I'm sure were hard for them. But I always knew that even though they didn't approve of what I did, they always loved me as a person.   —Robert age 25

WHEN THE CHICKS COME HOME, THIS TIME WITH THEIR OWN BROOD

In my travels around the country I have the privilege of hearing a lot of stories from women like you and me. I carry tissues in my bag, ready to be pulled out for the women who share their stories and for myself. There's just no getting around it: Raising kids is not easy. I don't care where you live, how much money you make, the level of your education, or if your ancestors came over on the *Mayflower*. Parenting is the great equalizer. I've not met a woman yet—and doubt I ever will—who held her baby for the first time and thought: "You're going to grow up, make terrible choices, and all but ruin your life and mine." No, we all gaze at our wiggling, crinkled miracles, hoping and praying for only the best for them.

But as life unfolds before us day after day, we all encounter circumstances, some of which we didn't dream would happen in a thousand years. We face problems, some on the scale of crises, and must choose how we will respond. A son who marries a woman we adamantly disapprove of was not what we planned. A daughter who finds herself living in an abusive situation happens only in made-for-TV movies, or so we thought. An adult child who moves back home with two children in tow to a house that was cramped before she left never crossed our minds.

A home is a kingdom of its own in the midst of the world, a stronghold amid life's storms and stresses, a refuge, even a sanctuary.
                                                    —Dietrich Bonhoeffer

---

Complicated situations such as these happen every day, and I don't pretend to understand the pain of every parent, grandparent, and child. But I do know that good can come from bad. Difficult circumstances can make us better people, and hard times can cement a family together in a way that nothing else can. As the parents of hurting adult children who are parents themselves, our reaction to painful problems makes a monumental difference.

A mother is the truest friend we have when trials, heavy and sudden, fall upon us; when adversity takes the place of prosperity.
                                                    —Washington Irving

---

A young woman told me a story and with her permission, I will share it with you. I was blessed by hearing it; I think you will be too.

Five years ago, against her parents' wishes, Beth married Raymond. For a while everything seemed to be going well for them. Raymond's dad had put him in charge of a part of the family restaurant business. Just before their second anniversary

Beth gave birth to their first child. Eighteen months later they had another child. Shortly afterward things began to fall apart.

Beth began to notice that Raymond was spending more and more time at work. As she later learned, he was spending more and more time with a woman he knew from his "old life" of doing drugs, a life Beth knew nothing about until now.

> *You may have a fresh start at any moment you choose, for this thing that we call "failure" is not the falling down, but the staying down.*
> —Mary Pickford

When Beth came home one day after picking the children up from Mothers' Day Out, she found Raymond in bed with this woman, both of them naked and passed out, with alcohol bottles and drug paraphernalia in plain view. Beth immediately packed as many belongings as she could, grabbed the two kids, and drove ten hours to her mother and father's home. She and her kids moved in with them.

"Their help was so practical," she told me. "They helped me find a lawyer, and they agreed to keep the kids while I was in legal meetings. They also helped me find a counselor to guide me in processing my emotions. In a few weeks, I felt settled in and the kids were in a routine. My parents and I agreed that I should stay with them until my divorce was final and my ex-husband started paying child support (the court gave me full custody). I found a part-time job, one that I could do from home, and in six months I was able to get an apartment of my own."

As Beth came to the end of her story, she told me that her parents insisted that she let them keep her kids a couple of times a week so that she could have time to do things for herself. That's how she ended up at my seminar. At the end of our short time together Beth said, "I don't know what I would have done without my parents' love and support. This is really what family is about."

A quote I saved from Pope John Paul II pretty much sums up Beth's story: "To maintain a joyful family requires much from both the parents and the children. Each member of the family has to become, in a special way, the servant of the others."

Without hearts there is no home.
—Lord Byron

As you can see from Beth's example, our reaction to the unexpected needs of our adult children can be pivotal in terms of their success and contentment. Never underestimate your contribution as a parent—and never expect it to be over. Life has a way of dealing us the most surprising cards, but you never know when you'll get a great hand. Keep playing with enthusiasm—and keep the porch light on.

If your child has moved back home, your once-clean house is a little littered, your phone rings more than once per day, and your schedule might include taking grandkids to the dentist. Yes, it's an adjustment, but consider the investment you're making in your relationships with your child and his or her children. Your being a good sport about the circumstances that caused your child to need your housing temporarily frees him or her to pursue correcting those circumstances—without your blame as baggage. And it lets your child know that unconditional love truly exists.

6

Keep Your Clan Connected

To us, family means putting your arms around each other and being there.
—Barbara Bush

On a recent trip to Colorado my husband and I attended an arts and crafts exhibit. As we strolled from booth to booth, admiring the work of local artisans, a painting caught our attention. It depicted three young Chinese cranes on their first flight. The artist told us that both the mother and the father help prepare the chicks for their beginning ascent and fly close to them during their initial migration south so that they can learn the route.

Give birth to them and nourish them. Give birth to them but don't try to own them. Help them to grow but don't rule them. This is called "Profound Virtue."
—Lao-tzu

We moved on to the next booth, but we continued to talk about how that painting reflected where we are in life. We've prepared our boys to leave the nest. We flew fairly close to them as they learned the ins and outs, ups and downs of life on their own. Now two of them are flying by themselves, with the third close behind. (By the way, we bought the painting.)

Now that for the most part our sons are soloing in the skies, our roles as parents have changed. We no longer guide them along the migration route, and they travel with other "flocks" now; in fact, they'll soon be building nests themselves. Bill and I have the new task of keeping our family in touch and close no matter how far away one member flies.

As our children leave home and our clan expands, maintaining and strengthening our relationship with them become ever more challenging. They have growing responsibilities and outside interests—careers, new friends, spouses, children, stepchildren—and we have waited until they were gone to pursue some new interests of our own. While we look to redefine our roles and ties with our adult children, we also must welcome the people they bring into our lives—spouses, in-laws, grandkids—and figure out how to nourish those relationships so that they also will grow and flourish in positive ways.

PAVING THE WAY FOR A LIFETIME OF HEALTHY RELATIONSHIPS

I received some wise advice from a longtime friend and mentor about maintaining healthy relationships with adult children. She told me several promises she made to her grown children and suggested that I think about them for my own. These promises can lay the foundation for staying connected and committed for a lifetime.

Using what my friend had written, I developed my own set of promises that I can live by as a mom. They spell out the commitment I maintain as a mother no matter what ages my sons are. (As you read these promises, you will want to contribute your own ideas and/or goals that make sense in your particular scenario.)

1. *I will give you the gift of boundaries, mine and yours.*
   I love your presence and enjoy being with you, but
   I will keep in mind that we both have our own lives
   to live. I will value your time, schedule, and responsibilities. I'll keep in touch regularly by e-mail, and
   I'll try to call to talk when it's convenient. I'll visit as
   often as I can, but I will make sure it's a good time
   for you before I come over. If you move away, when
   I visit, I won't overstay my welcome. I will try to be a
   helpful house guest, respecting the way you run your
   home and life. It's your home, and so I won't ask
   intrusive questions or criticize the way you do things.
   In the same spirit, I will keep you up to date on my
   schedule and responsibilities. I will appreciate the
   fact that you value my time and are as punctual as
   possible at the times we arrange to get together.
   I will gladly make room in my schedule whenever
   I can and be available whenever I can to help you.
   But I'll be honest with you about times I can't help
   you with a project or with baby-sitting. I will respect
   your need for alone and personal family time.

2. *I will assume your life is yours.* I believe that God has
   made you with special abilities and talent, and so
   I will support your career decisions and/or changes.
   I will not interfere with your decisions in choosing
   where you live or how you spend your money.
   I won't push my desires on you, insert myself into
   your family life, or try to squeeze you into a mold of
   my making. In the same vein, I won't make your life
   my life. Although I am proud to be your mother,
   I won't gain all my significance from you. I will
   maintain a life of my own. I will not get my identity

or contentment from your behavior, lifestyle, or achievements.

3. *I will always love you unconditionally.* I won't stop caring for you and your well-being. I may not agree with all your choices and may feel pain over some of the consequences of your choices, but I will always love you. I will always respect your right to make your own decisions. I will always be immensely proud of you, even if the wonderful person you are is not shining through at certain times.

I have been given the greatest gift by two wonderful parents: unconditional love.

—George W. Bush

---

4. *I will be a listening ear and a person you can trust.* I will listen and give advice—if you ask for it. I will try to keep my mouth shut when you don't want my counsel. I won't say "I told you so" if things don't turn out the way you hoped. Neither will I tell your problems to all my friends. I won't be the family gossip or go-between. I won't play favorites. I will keep your secrets secret and your dreams in my prayers.

5. *I will respect the way you decide to raise your children.* I won't bother you with nagging reminders about the way I raised you. I will be fair to you and your children in the gifts I give. I won't try to insert my opinion on family matters through the children. I won't assume the care of your household and family. I won't criticize your style of living. Even though I hope that you will carry on some of our family tra-

ditions, I won't expect you to follow every rule and ritual from your childhood. I will respect your methods of discipline when your children are in my home. I will shower them with the same love and support I gave you. I will strive to be a good role model for them, exemplifying positive character qualities and strong values in the way I live my life.

In the all-important world of family relations, three words are almost as powerful as the famous "I love you." They are "Maybe you're right."

—Oren Arnold

---

6. *I will pray for you in your adult life.* I will not try to force my beliefs on you or expect you to believe exactly the way I do. I will respect the way you handle spiritual matters in your own home. I won't assume that you will follow my spiritual path.

7. *I will be responsible for my own life.* I will consult you when planning for my senior years. I will keep you abreast of my plans for the future. I will make you aware of my will and the broad parameters of its contents. I won't use your inheritance to control you.

When we were married less than two years and had only one child, a job halfway across the country beckoned. It took us away from our hometown, where we had been surrounded by wonderful family and friends—people we had known all our lives. We adjusted slowly to our new hometown, made friends, and started a fresh network of security.

Though at first the change scared us, in looking back we have to conclude that the move away from our security base was the best thing that ever happened to us as a couple. It made us depend more on each other and develop new skills in life. We finally had to grow up into adulthood and leave our childhood support system. We became acquainted with each other in richer and deeper ways.

Now it is my turn to wave good-bye graciously to my grown children. It is their chance to finish growing up in ways they never can if they stay close by. I make the long trips to see them, and I always enjoy discovering the ways they have matured into the special adults they are. They really are grown-ups now. They have established their own places on this planet.

—Martha, age 61

MAKING IN-LAWS INTO FAMILY

Being a great mother for a lifetime is a delicate balancing act that entails knowing when to get involved and when to pull back, when to offer help and when to keep one's mouth shut. It involves learning to love new people and accept them into the family. It demands purposeful caring and cautious counseling. It also requires that I fulfill the role that usually falls to moms to be the nexus of family communication: the one who brings the scattered members together and keeps them informed about each other's happenings.

When a son or daughter marries, you suddenly have new in-laws who directly and indirectly influence your child. The prospect of all this change—of gaining a son- or daughter-in-law and embarking on a relationship with his or her parents—

can be intimidating. Yet even though you begin as strangers, mutual respect, consideration, and communication will help maintain a cordial and growing relationship, one that is cemented by a common commitment to the welfare of your children and grandchildren. Here are some ways to begin making connections with your counterparts:

- Find out how they celebrate special occasions in their family.

- Show genuine interest in their family traditions.

Without a family, man, alone in the world, trembles with the cold.

—Andre Malreaux

- Take a lot of pictures with them included. E-mail or mail them copies.

- Take a trip together. Start small: an afternoon of lunch and visiting something or somewhere that interests you both.

- Explore the hobbies you have in common; show an interest in ones new to you.

- If your in-laws are from a different culture, learn about it. A friend whose son was engaged to a girl from another country wisely researched the family and wedding traditions and holiday celebrations of that country. In addition to searching the Internet and reading books, she called that country's embassy in Washington, D.C., and received a lot of helpful information.

- Tell your in-laws how much you appreciate their child. Be specific about some of the positive qualities you've noticed: "Brad has a confident presence when he meets new people." "Anna has done a wonderful job of making their apartment warm and welcoming."

No matter how many communes anybody invents, the family always creeps back.

—Margaret Mead

- Coordinate schedules so that your kids can spend time easily with both families. Remember, your children can't be in two places at the same time, so don't put unreasonable pressure on them to adhere to your schedule and traditions.

BE A GREAT IN-LAW

"No word arouses more awe and dread amongst primitive people than the word *mother-in-law*," according to Sir James George Frazer, a nineteenth-century anthropologist. This doesn't have to be the case. You can take steps to make sure that you are a welcome presence to your child's spouse. The process takes time and demands sensitivity, with respect for the other person's privacy. Of course, it helps a lot if your son- or daughter-in-law shows equal determination and effort. But that's not always the case, and you can control only your part of the relationship. Don't underestimate how much good you can do toward keeping the relationship positive and growing. Here are some ways to do that:

- Get to know the person with whom your child has fallen in love. Look for that person's good points, accomplishments, and interests.

- Talk with your daughter- or son-in-law about what you want to be called. Ask for his or her input about what feels comfortable: your first name, Mom, Mother? Try to agree on a name that encourages the relationship.

- Treat him or her as a peer. Just as you would get your house ready and offer beverages and foods for your visiting friends, do the same thing for your child and his wife (see "Making Your Home a Magnet" in Chapter 5).

- Learn the favorite foods and special tastes of your daughter- or son-in-law. Keep his or her favorite beverages and snacks around the house.

- Don't make assumptions about what he or she needs. Wait to be asked to help.

- Make sure your home is visitor-friendly. Check the condition of your guest bed if you have one. Sleep in it one night. If you're not comfortable, no one else will be. Consider putting a new bed in your budget. What about the pillows? Old, musty ones can trigger allergies and cause discomfort.

- Offer to pay for creating a guest room or comfortable guest quarters at their home. If their home is small, offer to buy a blow-up bed. The idea is to make it as easy as possible for them to have you as a guest and for you to feel good about where you'll stay in their home.

- When you're visiting their home, take along things that will make your visit a little easier, such as your own pillow or something to read so that the couple don't feel they have to entertain you all the time. And don't stay too long.

- Be a good guest. Offer to help in the kitchen and wash your linens and towels if you stay overnight. Pitch in in unobtrusive ways: Pick up a dish when you're walking through the family room and put it in the dishwasher, fold throws and straighten sofa pillows before going to bed, fold a load of towels while you're watching television.

- Never criticize your son or daughter in front of his or her mate. Never criticize your son- or daughter-in-law in front of your child.

- Don't intervene with the couple's financial issues. Don't ask questions or give unsolicited advice.

It is with advice as with taxation: we can endure very little of either, if they come to us in the direct way.
—Sir Arthur Helps

- Offer to work on a project together, such as painting a room or planting flowers in their yard.

- If you are living under the same roof, keep your sense of humor, be flexible, and respect each other's privacy. Set reasonable house rules for cleaning and clutter, create guidelines for financial arrangements, and talk openly about what each person needs most to make this work.

- Confront problems with family members in private. Try to set a time when the two of you can spend time alone. Talk about how you feel, not about how you want the other person to change. If your son-in-law makes insensitive comments, say, "It hurts me to hear

you say things like that about our family. Is there something that's coloring your attitude I don't know about?"

- Sometimes you have to set limits or take a firm stand
on an issue. Communicate in a kind, nonblaming
way if you're starting to feel resentful or taken advantage of: "I love keeping the baby, but please call and
give me a couple of days' notice so that I can see if
baby-sitting fits into that day's schedule."

- Remember, no one person always gets his or her way
in a family. Be willing to compromise. If both you
and your daughter-in-law's family have the tradition
of opening presents on Christmas morning and then
having a big breakfast, maybe you could offer to open
presents at your house late Christmas afternoon and
have a big dinner afterward.

---

*If you can't get rid of the family skeleton, you may as
well make it dance.*

—George Bernard Shaw

- Keep your sense of humor. One new bride's mother-
in-law commented about how many hair products she
kept in the shower almost every time she dropped by
their house, implying that her daughter-in-law didn't
need that many and should weed them out. "Finally, I
just laughed and told her to be glad she didn't have to
shower in there," the daughter-in-law said.

- Never put your child in the position of having to
choose between allegiance to you and allegiance to his
or her mate.

- In short, treat your new son- or daughter-in-law the way you would like to be treated—as a special, loved person.

HOW TO BE THE WORST IN-LAW EVER

We can learn from bad examples as well as from good ones. Like me, you probably have witnessed or heard stories about some nightmarish in-law situations that have colored your perspective and expectations. For all of us who value our families, who want to stay connected as they expand, there are three things we should go to great lengths to avoid—surefire ways to be a bad in-law.

1. *Be critical.* Make derogatory comments about how your new son- or daughter-in-law is incompetent or ignorant because he or she has ideas, preferences, or ways of doing things that are different from yours. Blame the in-law for any problems your son, daughter, or grandchildren experience. When they make mistakes, say, "I told you so."

   Better: Remember that just as no one is perfect, neither is anyone all bad. Give your child's spouse the benefit of the doubt. If you see characteristics that concern you or if you don't feel good about him or her, trust your judgment but give that person a chance to show his or her other facets. Realize that everyone in the world does not share your philosophies, preferences, and political views—and that's okay. Look for things on which you can agree. Look for what he or she is doing right instead of focusing on what he or she is doing differently—or wrong—in your eyes.

2. *Be consuming and controlling.* Expect your children and their families to be totally involved with you. Nose your way into their affairs, ask intrusive questions, and expect them to tell you everything. Be ever-present in their lives and affairs. Treat your child and new in-law as if they are incapable of handling their own lives and step in to do it better. Offer love and cooperation only when they do a good job of pleasing you. Manipulate them to do things your way. Pile on guilt when they don't do what you think they should.

   Better: Give young marrieds the space and time to "leave and cleave." Even if you and your daughter have been very close, realize that it is healthy for her to forge her own way and define her own family. Respect her and her husband's privacy. Allow them the freedom to turn down requests or invitations that conflict with their plans or priorities. Don't push your opinions or give unsolicited advice. Wait for your kids to ask. Let them figure things out for themselves. Sure, sometimes they'll make mistakes that will cost them an arm and a leg, but the lessons can be valuable and character-building.

No matter how old a mother is, she watches her middle-aged children for signs of improvement.

—Florida Scott-Maxwell

---

3. Be personally needy. Neglect caring for yourself. Allow the consequences and chaos of your own personal issues—addictions, marital conflicts, emotional prob-

lems, financial issues—to affect your child's family. Be dependent on your children for help and support.

Better: There are times in all of our lives when we need the help and support of the family. That's what a family is for. But the extreme case is people who won't take responsibility for their own lives, who have a destructive, draining effect on everyone around them. Instead, we should take responsibility for our own lives. We need to learn to maintain ourselves as we grow older, give high priority to our self-care and well-being. Part of nurturing ourselves is seeking professional help to resolve issues that drag us and our extended families down.

You must do the thing you think you cannot do.
                                    —Eleanor Roosevelt

If you're having trouble coping with daily life and relationships, get the help you need from a physician, therapist, clergyperson, financial counselor, or self-help organization such as Alcoholics Anonymous. Needing help with your life does not make you a weak person, but needing help, not seeking it, and allowing it to affect others in destructive ways make you an unwise person.

TOUCHY ISSUES

It happens in the best of families. People feel hurt, criticized, unloved, rejected. Words alone can't break bones, but when delivered harshly, they can break hearts. Unfortunately, criticism is a toxin that works its way into many families, creating resentment, hard feelings, and depression. Criticism is never constructive. Instead, the best way to change the behavior you find objectionable in someone else is to work on yourself first.

It is much easier to be critical than to be correct.
—Benjamin Disraeli

If you catch yourself criticizing your son- or daughter-in-law, stop immediately. Since you are the parent and the older and presumably more mature person in the relationship, your response can go a long way toward creating a good atmosphere in which healing and forgiveness can take place and love can grow. Avoiding criticism—no, on second thought, building a strong fortress against it—should be something everyone in your family takes very seriously. If you have an in-law who is being critical of you, look deeper inside yourself and try to discover how you might be contributing to the problem. Ask yourself some tough questions, such as the following:

- Is there anything you are aware of that has offended your son- or daughter-in-law?

- Have you been unreasonable in your expectations about how often they will call or visit you, where they will spend holidays, what kind of gifts they will give you, or how you want to be treated?

- Have you been critical or judgmental?

- Have you been respectful of their privacy, or have you been intrusive?

- Have you been impatient or even rude?

- Have you shown compassion and unconditional love?

- Have you *really* listened and tried to understand why your son- or daughter-in-law is upset with you?

We find comfort among those who agree with us—growth among those who don't.
—Frank A. Clark

The next time angry words or looks signal that conflict is bubbling over, take a few steps to defuse and understand the situation:

- First, stop what you are doing and look directly in the eyes of your critic. Actively listen to what he or she is saying. If you are on the phone, affirm that you are listening. Don't interrupt. Let your in-law talk.

- Try to listen between the lines—discern what is going on behind the remarks. It could be that you are the object of pent-up frustration or hormones.

- Realize and accept the fact that the criticism is your in-law's perspective, what she believes to be correct. Therefore, it doesn't do any good to make accusations about your in-law being oversensitive or irrational. If the criticism is exaggerated, don't get hung up trying to correct him or her on the spot.

- Don't evade the issue or bring up another topic. Deal with it.

- Don't make fun of the criticism, as it may be a sensitive issue from your in-law's perspective. Besides, poking fun at it will make you look sarcastic and belittling.

- Try to remain open to finding truth in it. Usually there is at least something valid, even if it's poppy-seed-size, in the critic's words.

Quarrels would not last long if the fault was only on one side.

—François de la Rochefoucauld

- After you've listened to the criticism, ask for an opportunity to respond. Begin by restating what you heard to make sure you understood it. Then share what you feel about the criticism and what you believe to be true. Share your thoughts and feelings in a calm manner. Most likely your relative will feel sorry for the effect of his or her remarks and think twice before criticizing you again.

Conflict cannot survive without your participation.

—Author unknown

Relationships are a two-way street, and sometimes one party refuses to meet in the middle. If you are trying to build a healthy relationship and your in-law is being uncooperative, realize that there are some cases in which no amount of talking will help. Your son- or daughter-in-law may be dealing with an underlying emotional or past family issue. If you find yourself continually hitting a brick wall trying to make the relationship work, consider seeking the advice of a family therapist or pastor who is trained to understand relational systems and continue to do your part.

Whatever response you receive from your efforts, you'll know you made loving efforts, and that will ease your guilt and pain if your in-law ultimately rejects your heartfelt attempts to build a positive relationship.

WAYS TO STAY CONNECTED

Whether your children live 2 or 2,000 miles away and whether they're single or married, with or without children, you can do some simple things to cement family ties:

- At least twice a year have each household in your extended family write up a page about what's happened in their lives, what they've been up to, and so on. Have them send the information to you or another designated family member so that you can combine them and send out copies to everyone.

- Create a family Web page. This is the age of on-line communication, and a Web page lets the whole family stay connected. As you or another computer-literate family member update the page with a daughter's promotion or a son's new car, everyone else can post congrats to each other.

- Consider getting an 800 number. For a minimal monthly charge you can make calling home easy and cost-free for your kids. This is a good investment, I think.

- Rent motel rooms near an adult child who is feeling alone or isolated, giving family members a place to play and swim together.

- Volunteer together for an organization or cause that allows you to share your combined talents and interests. One family I know meets every summer at a designated mission or relief effort. For a week they donate their time and energy. The second week they vacation someplace nearby.

• If your young adult lives with or near you, celebrate an accomplishment or life change—large or small— with the honoree's favorite meal and a toast: "To Melissa, the best new teacher in the district." "To Josh, the son we're so proud of. Here's to your success at your new job." "To Sally; we've been blessed to have you for eighteen years at home. Here's to your achievement in college."

It isn't the big pleasures that count the most; it's making a great deal out of the little ones.

—Jean Webster

• When your kids come home for a visit, "just happen" to have the photo albums out on the coffee table or kitchen counter. Enjoy looking through them together. Plan one night to gather and watch family videos and look through scrapbooks.

• Send a present that's not for any particular holiday and has personal significance. My husband's aunt invited me to lunch and gave me one of her silver serving dishes just because she wanted me to have it. She has gone out of her way to make me feel like a part of her side of the family, and that makes me feel very special. I want to follow her example when I have the opportunity.

- Kids never grow too old for games. Sometimes it just takes someone to make the suggestion to play Scrabble, Tripoly, or Trivial Pursuit. Next time the kids are at your house, have the games handy.

- Buy DVDs or videos of favorite family movies (start a collection) so that you can enjoy them when you're all together. When all the boys are at our house, they always want to watch *Gladiator* and *Braveheart*. At Christmas we always watch *It's a Wonderful Life*.

People need joy quite as much as clothing. Some of them need it far more.

—Margaret Collier Graham

- Write a journal of your memories to pass on to your child. When you come across old photos or memoirs, give them to your child. For years my mother has made an extra effort to bring me an old photograph or letter each time she comes to visit. The letters she saved when I was in college and photos from family vacations and occasions are dear to me.

- Start a family gratitude book. Years ago, after the Thanksgiving meal, we started recording things for which we were thankful. It's fun to look back and see our entries from ten years back—even from one year ago. This Thanksgiving try it yourself. It will be a blessing in years to come.

- Start a tradition of having family appreciation time. Fix your favorite foods. Turn off the phone's ringer (turn off cell phones too) and settle down for a confab. Have each family member say what he or she appreciates about other family members. We did this now and then when all five of us were living together, and we do it now at the end of a vacation or holiday week. It's a very meaningful time, especially for us as the parents, to hear each boy say what he values about the others now that they are older.

We have left undone those things which we ought to have done; and we have done those things which we ought not to have done.

—The Book of Common Prayer

- If you have extended family close by, you might start a tradition of always spending certain holidays or occasions—Memorial Day, Fourth of July, Labor Day, birthdays—together. Life transitions and religious rituals such as baptisms, confirmations, and mitzvahs can become occasions for sharing and celebration.

- Housewarmings don't have to be only an excuse to give and receive gifts; they can be an initiation of a house becoming a home. Celebrate this with your family.

- Revive some old family traditions by getting together for Sunday suppers, outings, games, sports, and other activities that have been enjoyed through the generations. When we realize we're doing something that our parents or grandparents did when they were children, it evokes feelings of continuity and security.

Sunday nights are a blast at our house. We call it family night. Our three kids, their spouses, and the grandkids come over around six o'clock. I fix an easy dinner that includes something the grandkids like. I plan something fun to do—a treasure hunt in the backyard, a simple craft—to keep the grandkids occupied while their parents and my husband sit around the table and discuss world events, books, and things like that.

Then we as a family sing songs around the piano. I keep a world map on the wall in the dining room (I've given up trying for decorator of the month) as well as a globe, and we spend a little time each week learning where countries are. We also keep a Bible memory verse going.

Maybe this sounds like something from an old black-and-white movie, but it's not. My husband and I are busy business owners. Our kids are doctors, lawyers, entrepreneurs, and parents. It's such fun for my husband and me to create an opportunity every week for us all to get off the fast track and enjoy the simple pleasures of being a family. It's a weekly reminder to us all of what's really important in life.

—Judie, age 55

THE GRANDDADDY OF ALL GET-TOGETHERS

An annual family reunion reminds everyone that you're in life together for the duration—and you're glad about it. It's fun to watch the changes from year to year in people's lives, especially the children. If you're the one who instigates events in your family, you may find yourself arranging it the first year. But as the tradition becomes popular, others will step in and help. Be sure to record everything—your research on locations, costs, what worked well and what didn't—for the person to whom you pass the baton.

> *No matter what you've done for yourself or for humanity, if you can't look back on having given love and attention to your own family, what have you really accomplished?*
>
> —Lee Iacocca

If you've never planned a family reunion, you may want to start on a small scale. For example, when we moved back to Texas three years ago after a sojourn in Tennessee, one of our priorities was to get together with Bill's extended family there. We wanted our boys to get to know their relatives at some occasion other than a funeral. The first year we hosted a dinner party for those who lived within a fifty-mile radius, and people of a whole range of ages attended: cousins with new babies and young children, high schoolers, even Bill's delightful eighty-something aunt who had more energy and pizzazz than anyone else there.

Tips for a Fun Gathering

- Appoint an interested family member to be a reunion journalist: He or she should collect historical information and interesting facts throughout the event. Afterward, gather this information into a family newspaper that commemorates the day. Print and distribute it to all who attended. Also consider compiling a family cookbook by having members bring their favorite recipes on index cards.

- Have each family member write a little-known fascinating fact about himself or herself on an index card. Collect the cards and have someone read each one out loud; see if players can identify who wrote them.

- An artistic family member can bring a large picture of a family tree. Allot time for folks to write their family's names on branches.

- Honor older family members. Have them describe the biggest world change of their lifetime, the happiest memory of their childhood, and the first home they remember.

- Set up a separate game and craft area for young children.

- Relive family history by reviewing family members' photo albums.

- At the day's end, award family members for having the least amount of hair, the worst sunburn, or the best laugh or for being the queen of potato salad.

- Assign three or more family members the job of photographing and videotaping the event. Have a tech-savvy family member be in charge of creating a family Web page to help the whole family stay connected.

- Ask relatives to clean out their attics and basements before the reunion and bring some items they would like to auction off. Let one older child serve as the auctioneer and another act as the cashier. Use the proceeds to defray the cost of next year's reunion.

CONNECTING VS. THE CLOCK

The clock dominates how we spend our days more than it did at any time in history. We have more activities to arrive at and more deadlines to meet. Maybe we baby boomers anticipated an easier, less hectic life when our kids left the nest, but that hasn't happened. If, understandably, you are already maxed out time- and energywise, the idea of being the family connector may sound like the straw that finally will break your back.

At the end of your life you will never regret not having one more test, not winning one more verdict, or not closing one more deal. You will regret time not spent with a husband, a child, or a parent.

—Barbara Bush

If only we could throw away our date books, walk away from our jobs, move to a condo on the beach or a cabin in the woods, we fantasize, we could spend time on important things such as keeping our family members close and in touch. We could work on repairing, rebuilding, reinforcing, reconnecting. The solution, however, is not in escaping; that's not realistic. At least part of the solution is reprioritizing, deciding how important this issue is to you and then taking some steps, maybe small ones at first, to keep the family connected.

7

How to Be a Really Great Grandparent

Becoming a grandparent is a second chance to put to use all the things you learned the first time. . . . It's all love and no discipline.
                                                    —Dr. Joyce Brothers

*R*emember when Grandma and Grandpa lived out at the family farm? You could find them at home most days, and they were an ever-ready source of baby-sitting, roast chicken dinners, Sunday drives to nowhere, and long, pleasant chats on the front porch.

Times have changed, and now we, the baby boomers, the do-my-own-thing generation, are becoming grandparents. But we are also European travelers, antique shoppers, graduate students, dedicated noncooks, and folks embarking on second careers. In short, we are not the same kinds of grandparents with whom we grew up.

But hold on: We may be even better.

At age fifty, we boomers are in our prime. We're the best educated, most active, and youngest older generation ever. Just as baby boomers redefined youth and changed the culture of our country through our music, movies, and morals in the 1960s, we are redefining what it means to grow older and what it means to be a grandparent. No rocking chairs, shuffleboard, or being called "Grandma" for us. We sit in the lotus position, attend spin classes, and want to be called Nana or Gigi or Sue-Sue. We bring energy and enthusiasm to this important and influential role. And we're a generation that likes to make a difference.

A sufficient measure of civilization is in the influence of good women.
—Emerson

So what can we do? We can love and encourage our families, something we shouldn't take lightly in a bruised and hurting world. A successful woman told me that alcoholic parents and welfare checks were part of growing up for her, but she had one stabilizing influence: a grandmother who adored her.

We also can provide roots. In a unique way grandparents have always had a special gift of passing on family memories. This conjures up visions of the time my grandmother told about how she and my mom waited in line in the snow to see *Gone with the Wind*. Maybe our stories are about how we camped out on the sidewalk all night in freezing weather so that we could get tickets to a Simon and Garfunkel concert. The point is that it's all history, and it links our kids to their heritage.

The walks and talks we have with our two-year-olds in red boots have a great deal to do with the values they will cherish as adults.
—Edith F. Hunter

Perhaps the greatest gift we can offer our grandchildren is the gift of time, not only as baby-sitters but as eager volunteers who are ready to show them the wonders of the world. Time invested returns priceless dividends in shared experiences and deepening friendships.

> According to the National Institute of Aging, there will be 80 million grandparents by the year 2005, and according to *American Demographics,* nearly half of them will be baby boomers.

WHY OUR GENERATION CAN BE
THE BEST GRANDPARENTS EVER

- We're fit and feel young, and so we can be active with our grandkids, taking them on trips and exposing them to new experiences.

- Because we're well educated, we highly value our grandchildren's education.

- Because many of us learned the hard way about companies' lack of loyalty—we worked faithfully for twenty-five years only to receive a pink slip when the stock fell—we see the importance of investing in family, not careers. Therefore, we can pour ourselves freely into loving our grandkids in ways we should have with our kids: nurturing their talents, listening to their thoughts, cheering their dreams.

- Because we feel good about ourselves, we can help promote a positive self-image and increase the self-esteem of grandchildren.

- Because we're stable, we can foster a sense of family unity whether the distance between us and our grandkids is a mile or a thousand miles.

- Because we grew up in a generation that revered peace and love, we can be sources of unconditional, nonjudgmental support and affection for our grandchildren.

GUIDELINES FOR GREAT GRANDPARENTING

As excited as we are about becoming grandparents, it's important to remember that the little tykes are not *our* children. No matter how grand or gracious our plans, we need to consult their parents before we give them money, plan trips, or take them to events. And we especially need to be sensitive to the goals and guidelines our children have set up for their children and how they want to discipline them.

> *Kind words can be short and easy to speak, but their echoes are truly endless.*
> —Mother Teresa

Remember the five parenting guidelines that helped us pave the way for a long-lasting, loving relationship with each of our boys? (See Chapter 1.) Interestingly, many of the folks to whom I talk say these ideas make for good grandparenting as well, although they're applied a little differently. Here are the guidelines and some ideas on how to put them into practice.

1. Be Fair

Don't make unreasonable demands on your kids' and grandkids' time and attention. Don't monopolize their time or expect them to spend holidays with you automatically as they once did. Understand their need to develop family traditions of their own and be sensitive to the fact that there are grandparents on the other side of the family who want to see them as well.

It's helpful to sit down with your child and his or her spouse and discuss this openly far in advance of holidays and special events. If the other in-laws have a tendency to monopolize them, don't allow yourself to get into a fight for your child's family's time and attention. Encourage your child to be firm about fairness and then back away to let him or her sort things out. Let your son or daughter know that your self-esteem or love for him or her is not riding on this decision.

But be aware of this: Generally speaking, women tend to be more intentional about relationships than men are. Taking the initiative to stay connected with people comes naturally to the female gender, perhaps because it arises from the nurturing instinct. This being the case, if you have a son, realize that his new wife may tend to gravitate automatically toward her mom and her childhood home at holidays. It's easy for relationships on the son's side of the family to decrease.

This is something Bill and I are very aware of and have already talked about to our boys. You can counteract this tendency, we believe, by doing a couple of things. First, make your son aware that in marriage he'll feel pulled between families, and his wife probably will lean toward spending time with hers.

Second, encourage your son to initiate family gatherings himself—at both family homes.

Third, make sure your home is a magnet, a place they want to come back to (see Chapter 5).

2. Be Firm

It's fun to indulge and spoil your grandkids somewhat, but be careful, as it can get out of hand. Don't tolerate disrespect from your grandkids toward you or their parents. For their welfare and sanity, your grandkids need to obey you and show adults regard.

Allowing grandchildren to be disrespectful to you can be dangerous to them and make their visits very unpleasant for you. Talk to your children about how they would like for you to correct or discipline their children. If you spanked your children when they were growing up, realize that because of heightened awareness of child abuse, parents today are sometimes unsure and sensitive about how and when to discipline their children. Discuss how to handle this issue and work together to help young ones grow and develop in positive ways.

> My in-laws have some ideas about child rearing that are very different from mine. They used to make me angry and ruin the holidays we spent with them. They wanted to slap my daughter's hand when she touched something she shouldn't. I don't believe in slapping. Grandparents raised their children the way they wanted to, but now they should let us raise our children the way we want to. It really helped when my husband talked to them, told them they were upsetting me, and asked them to respect our views. He told them that they could reprimand or put our daughter in a time-out chair. Things are still a little awkward when we visit, but it's better than it used to be.
>
> —Christine, age 32

3. Be Fun

Many entertaining things vie for our kids' and grandkids' attention, and so their thinking of time with Nana and Bubby as a highlight of their lives is not a given. It's important to ask ourselves: "Do they want to get together with us, or do they dread being with us? Is coming to visit a fun thing?" Put making memories with your grandchildren high on your priority list. Get into their world and orchestrate activities they will enjoy. Plan occasions and events to celebrate the special moments of life and create and carry on family traditions. But make sure that you aren't so overwhelmed trying to do it "right" that you don't have any fun. Lighten up and enjoy them. They'll go home at the end of the day or week.

My dad is the boss until Grandma comes over. Then he's just one of us.

—A 5-year-old child

I know a man who loves his grandkids very much, but their time with Grandpa is serious business. He teaches and corrects their every move. Even when something is supposed to be a fun event, they can't ever seem to do it right, and that contaminates a lot of really fun opportunities.

4. Be Flexible

The only constant in life is change; children are predictably unpredictable. Those well-worn adages are still as true as ever. Accept the fact that calamity and confusion are a part of having young children around. Do yourself and your family a favor by finding humor in the inevitable mishaps and disappointments that plague every visit.

The greatest part of our happiness or misery depends on our dispositions and not on our circumstances.

—Martha Washington

You don't want your life to revolve around them, but don't be so rigid that you can't enjoy a spontaneous visit or a change in plans. Roll with the punches and don't let unexpected situations keep you from enjoying the opportunities you have.

Be sensitive to the fact that children are constantly growing. Their abilities and interests change regularly. Stay abreast of their needs and developmental levels. What you may think is a wonderful, educational toy or outing may be too advanced for your grandchild. However, you want to avoid boring them as well.

5. Be Affirming

Every human being, no matter her age, needs to be reminded of her value—her innate worth. We also need to be reminded of our uniqueness and the contribution we can make—how we are making a difference in the world. Expressing to a child his potential greatness brings out the best in him.

The supreme happiness of life is the conviction that we are loved.

—Victor Hugo

As a grandparent we're in a position to—and almost are expected to—lavish exuberant praise on our grandchildren. What would have seemed braggadocio with our own children is perfectly acceptable coming from a grandparent. We have a unique opportunity to affirm and influence strong self-esteem in our grandchildren. What a beautiful gift we can give them.

Affirming our children in their parenting role is powerful as well. Applauding your daughter's new mothering techniques—"I never thought to soothe a baby that way. What a great idea!" "I can see this baby loves her mom"—goes a long way toward building her confidence, and that will make her a better mom.

PREPARING FOR YOUR NEW ROLE

To be a good grandparent, you need to know what to expect. If you haven't been around babies for two or three decades, believe me, a lot has changed. Prenatal testing, which many of us had never heard of, is now routine. Pregnancy norms have relaxed. A really good friend of mine is an OB/GYN, and she says that depending on the size of the mother, many gain between twenty-five and thirty-five pounds, and some doctors allow even more. And mothers to be are encouraged to keep playing tennis or attending aerobics classes if they've been doing that regularly.

> *What feeling is so nice as a child's hand in yours? So small, so soft and warm, like a kitten huddling in the shelter of your clasp.*
>
> —Marjorie Holmes

Most mothers now can learn the sexes of their babies before birth. Most babies are born today in birthing rooms, and some at birthing centers—instead of a cold, sterile operating room—where family members can share the event. Some hospitals have midwives on staff for mothers who prefer that approach. Before the blessed event a mom can develop a "birth plan" and meet with a "lactation consultant."

In short, we don't know it all. We need to get up to speed, read the books our kids are reading to prepare for parenting, ask our daughters to bring us copies of free brochures from their doctors' offices, and become familiar with new products and equipment for babies: Boppys, Snuglis, Diaper Genies, and the like. Here are some terms to know:

Amniocentesis. This is a test given to mothers who are over thirty-five or have a history of gene-linked diseases or other problems and those whose earlier test results were abnormal. A doctor takes a small sample of fluid by inserting a long, ultrathin needle through the abdomen and into the amniotic sac. The doctor uses ultrasound before and during the procedure to guide the needle in order to avoid the fetus and placenta. By analyzing the fluid doctors can detect neural defects, Down's syndrome, and other genetic disorders. They also can determine the sex of the baby.

Birthing center. Many hospitals have birthing rooms that look more like hotel suites than hospital rooms. Rather than moving from place to place, the mother stays in this room, known as the LDR (labor, delivery, recovery) or sometimes the LDRP (labor, delivery, recovery, postpartum) room. The staff comes to her, wheeling the necessary equipment in and out. Family members are allowed to be in the room.

Birth plan. Some hospitals allow the mother to prepare a birth plan with her preferences stated in advance, which can include things such as pain medication and whether she will have an epidural.

Lactation consultant. This person has been trained and certified to help mothers breast-feed successfully.

Sonogram. A sonogram is an image of the fetus created by ultrasound. The test is given commonly to mothers, usually between the sixteenth and eighteenth weeks of pregnancy. Doctors use it to calculate the age and condition of the fetus, predict the due date, detect multiple fetuses, and show any serious visible abnormalities. It also can reveal the sex of the fetus.

Triple screen. This is a common blood test expectant mothers take, usually between weeks fifteen and twenty, that measures three substances produced by the fetus and placenta: AFP (alpha-fetoprotein), hCG (human chorionic gonadotropin), and estriol. Low or high levels of these substances can indicate neural-tube and other structural defects and genetic disorders such as Down's syndrome.

WHEN A NEW GRANDBABY COMES ALONG

The day a baby arrives is a joyous one, and family members near and far love to herald the birth of a brand-new human being in their midst. Grandparents can be a big help—or a big hindrance—during this special event. The key is being sensitive to what the parents want and need.

A new baby is like the beginning of all things—wonder, hope, a dream of possibilities.

—Eda J. Le Shan

Here are some tips for grandparents regarding the wants and needs of children who have just become parents:

- Ask whether—don't assume—the new parents will want you in the waiting room, in the delivery room, or at home when they return with the baby. Comply graciously with their wishes regardless of what you'd like.

- Don't voice your opinion if you don't like what they named the baby.

- Respect the new mother's need to bond with her child.

- Take lots of pictures and share them with relatives who can't be on hand.

- Offer to supply some frozen casseroles for after the baby arrives so that the family won't have to cook at that busy, exhausting time.

- Communicate with the other grandparents about visits to avoid misunderstandings and friction.

- Show some extra affection to the baby's siblings, who may feel overlooked. A wonderful book to give an older brother or sister is either *I'm the Big Sister* or *I'm the Big Brother* by Susan Russell Ligon (Tommy Nelson, 2002).

- Offer to do laundry, run errands, and chauffer older kids to their various commitments while their parents are consumed with the new arrival.

- Don't drop in without calling.

- Tell the parents how grateful you are for this new little life.

- Don't bombard them with advice. Of course you know the baby is tired, hungry, or wet, but the parents will figure it out on their own soon enough.

- If the baby is fussy or has trouble sleeping, don't keep telling them how good all your babies were.

- Give the gift of your time. If you live in the same area, offer to baby-sit one night a week so that they can go out. Or offer to help your daughter-in-law do spring cleaning since it's hard for her to do that with a baby underfoot.

- Keep learning about how to be a good grandparent; www.aarp.org and www.grandsplace.com are good resources.

GRANDPARENTING ACROSS THE MILES

In these days of scattered extended families, it's common to have miles and hours between you and your grandchildren. The good news is that you can still be a vital presence in their lives between visits as well as when get-togethers are possible. Here are some ways to build strong and loving relationships with little ones who live at a distance.

- Make sure your grandkids have a good photo of you placed where even the youngest ones can see it regularly.

- Read some of the books your grandkids are reading. You'll have an automatic conversation starter.

- Record yourself reading books for young grandchildren. They'll learn to know your voice.

- Phone at a regular time monthly or weekly. Letter writing works too.

- "Visit" often via e-mail. By the time a child is four or five, he or she probably will be learning and playing games on a computer. Once a child is able to read, there is no better instant, economical way to stay in touch.

- Consider writing a story with an older child: Each one of you writes a paragraph and mails or e-mails it to the other to work on.

- Begin the habit of talking on the phone to even a grandchild who can't talk back yet.

- Find out game schedules for older, sports-minded grandkids. Let them know you'll be cheering come game time even if you can't attend in person. The same goes for grandkids with musical interests.

- On a weekend visit or trip work with older grandkids to make a scrapbook or journal of the time you spend together.

- Take up a hobby together, perhaps gardening or photography. You can exchange seeds and/or photos.

- Arrange a win/win situation: Offer to baby-sit for a weekend. You get grandkid time, and the parents get a much-needed break.

Before your grandkids come for a visit, find out their preferences in an e-mail or letter. Ask what cereals, lunch foods, beverages, and snacks they like, as well as what their bedtimes and usual wake-up times are. What kind of pillow do they like? What are they allowed to watch on television? What would they like to do for fun?

When the family gathers, consider spending quality time with each grandchild.

- Take a grandchild to visit a place he or she is studying in school.

- Holidays can be too busy and stressful to allow for quality time with the grandkids. Arrange to attend an event that's less showy but still important to a grand-child: a school play, a children's choir concert, a mid-week soccer game.

- Remember your grandchildren's special dates: birth-days, holidays, special school programs, and extracur-ricular activities. Mark those days with cards and small gifts or a phone call.

- Perhaps you can afford to sponsor a grandchild in sport or activity his parents can't quite fit into their budget. Ask sensitively whether the parents would allow you to participate in this way.

- Let the kids teach you games when you're together. Enjoy time with them doing what they like.

- Make family a financial priority. Set aside money each month for phone calls and, if possible, visits.

- Let your grandkids know you are always available. Give them a phone card or get an 800 number they can use just for calling you.

For more information, contact the Foundation for Grandparenting at www.grandparenting.org and the Grand-parents' Website within Cyberparent.com at www.cyber parent.com/gran.

DIVORCE AND GRANDPARENTS

Much as we dread it, we know that some of our children will experience divorce. The statistics are all too familiar: According to the U.S. Census Bureau and the Stepfamily Foundation, one of every two marriages ends in divorce and 50 percent of children in the United States will go through a divorce before they are eighteen.

It's been said that grandparents are the other victims of divorce. If your adult child ends his marriage, you probably will experience some of the same feelings as your grandchild: anger over the situation, helplessness over events out of your control, anxiety about what the future holds, and sadness over your broken family.

Life is what we make it, always has been, always will be.
—Grandma Moses

Here are tips marriage and family therapists suggest to help you navigate the troubled waters:

- *Soothe the hurt.* Remember that this is a very painful time for your grandchild; she needs your love, support, and understanding. Focus your attention on her, not the parents.

- *Comfort the worrier.* Most children believe they are in some way responsible for their parents' divorce. This can lead to poor self-esteem. Use this time to encourage your grandchild. Be alert for ways to build him up and praise him.

- *Be a trustworthy listener.* Invite your grandchild to open up and express the way she honestly feels. Don't condemn or criticize her.

- *Be available.* Phone, e-mail, or visit regularly. Let him know you're always there for him. Ask him how you can help. Your time means the world to him.

- *Don't take sides.* Avoid making comments that could further damage the child's relationship with either parent.

- *Keep promises.* Your reliability is an enormous issue for a little child whose home has just split in two.

- *Be honest.* But don't feel you have to tell him everything, especially sordid details he doesn't need to know.

- *Show compassion.* Remind her that although her parents are angry at each other, they still love her, and so do you. Help her understand that she doesn't have to stop loving one parent in order to love the other.

- *Keep your relationship fun.* Orchestrate some positive, pleasurable experiences for your child. Help him get his mind on other things.

- *Stay in touch.* If your child's divorce threatens to separate you from your grandchildren, you may have legal recourse. First try to work out visits; if the divorced spouse won't cooperate, contact a lawyer about your right to see your grandchildren. Some states have laws mandating grandparent visitation if it's in the child's best interest. For more information, contact Grandparents United for Children's Rights, 137 Larkin Street, Madison, WI 53705; telephone 608-238-8751; e-mail sedun@inxpress.net.

- *Get any help you need.* If circumstances demand that you care for the children, get informed about what this entails. The AARP Grandparent Information Center is a good place to start: www.aarp.org/con-facts/programs/gic.html.

MAKING HISTORY MATTER

You can provide an invaluable resource for your grandchildren about their family roots, milestones, and turning points by telling them your story. Writing your autobiography is a great exercise for a couple of reasons: First, it connects your grandchildren to their past and gives them pride in the family name. Second, it helps you "sort your attic": revisit the years gone by and let go of old conflicts and occurrences that no longer matter.

In order to be in touch with someone else you must first be in touch with yourself.

—Michael J. Gelb

Writing your story isn't an overnight project. It's a process. You might set a goal of working on it an hour each week. Collect stories from family members and pull out your high school scrapbook and old photo albums. Organize your story around the themes of your life. Don't be discouraged if your grandchildren are not interested in the family history right now. It's still a good idea to pull memories and mementos together for later, when they may find them fascinating. One way to approach the writing of your family history is to answer the following groups of questions to determine what is worth recording:

Big Turning Points

- What events and experiences altered the direction of my life in a big way?

- When did those events occur? Which people were involved? What emotions do I remember about each event? How was my life changed?

Family

- Which family members played a major role in shaping my life? How did they do that?

- What is it about my childhood years and family that would help someone better understand how I became the person I am?

- What did I like best and least about my family?

- What were the major crises and conflicts?

- What were the stated and unstated rules?

- What family recipes have been handed down and by whom?

- What special skills did my parents or another relative teach me?

Activities, Education, and Friends

- What was school like in my day? What subjects did I study? How was school then different from school today?

- What were my best and worst teachers like?

- What outside activities did I participate in? Was I athletic or brainy or both?

- What was my favorite book? School subject? School activity?

- Did I have an active social life? What did kids do for fun then?

- Who were my best friends in elementary and high school? Am I in touch with any of those people today?

Career

- When I was a child, what did I want to be when I grew up?

- How did I end up in the work I am doing today?

- What have been my major disappointments and successes?

- What have I most enjoyed about various jobs?

We are always telling 'em [young people] what we used to not do. We didn't do it because we didn't think of it. We did everything we could think of.

—Will Rogers

Love

- What persons, places, and things did I love as a child?

- Who was my first love?

- When and where was my first date?

- What role has love played in my life?

- How have I expressed love to others?

- How have others expressed their love to me?

Health

- What was my health like as a baby, child, adolescent, and adult?

- Was I ahead of or behind others in development?

- How have I handled health problems?

- What have I done to improve my health?

Faith and Religion

- Was attending church, synagogue, or another place of worship part of my childhood? If so, which one did I attend and why?

- If attending religious services was a family tradition, would I have gone if I hadn't had to?

- Did I pray then? Do I pray today?

- What did I believe about God when I was young? Have I learned anything since then?

- How important is faith to daily life?

Grandkids don't need to know everything to get a sense of connectedness with the past. Don't bring out old "dirty laundry": ugly details about past conflicts. You don't have to whitewash your memories, but you don't have to let the bad parts contaminate the good ones either. Protect the minds, hearts, and feelings of your grandchildren by leaving out as much bad stuff as you can. They'll never miss it.

MAKING HISTORY LAST

If you have family mementos—uniforms, certificates of baptism or naturalization, heirlooms—gathering dust somewhere, get them out. Invite an interested grandchild to help you organize, label, store, or display them. Write down the stories—perhaps have your grandchild type them up on the computer for legibility—that go with each piece. Here are some other ideas:

- Consider making a scrapbook of smaller historical items with a grandchild.

- Let the grandkids choose some old photos they would like copies of and then get the copies made.

- Compile a cookbook of favorite family recipes. Start a tradition of helping your grandchild make one of these dishes for each holiday (or more often).

- Put old home movies on videotape for easier viewing. Consider making it a real movie project: For the soundtrack, ask older relatives to share the family history and play music appropriate to the times. Let the grandkids participate in the moviemaking as much as they want; give them copies of the finished product.

- Let grandchildren gather oral histories from older adults. Help them list interview questions and provide a tape recorder.

- Visit a museum with your grandchildren that reflects the time frame in which you grew up. Or take your grandkids to your childhood home or town. Show them where you played.

- Ask a tech-savvy grandchild to store precious photos on a computer disk or CD-ROM.

- Plan a kid-friendly family reunion. Show grandkids pictures of the relatives they can expect to see there.

- Have grandkids create a family museum somewhere in your home. Let them select the items that should be in it and arrange them. Then declare them "tour guides" and have them show and explain the display to other family members.

- Work with an older grandchild to research and record your family tree. Consider displaying photos with the tree.

- When remembering and remarking on family members and events, make sure you accentuate the positive. Your grandchild can learn a healthy, happy way of looking at life from you.

For more information, consider these resources:

My History Is America's History. A project of the National Endowment for the Humanities, this Web site provides a wealth of information, including a guidebook for tracing family history, a venue for exchanging family stories, and guidelines for preserving family treasures, among other resources. URL: www.myhistory.org.

The Library of Congress. This site contains one of the world's premier collections of U.S. and foreign genealogical and local historical publications. URL: lcweb.loc.gov/rr/genealogy/.

The National Archives (NARA). The National Archives and Records Administration provides this Web site for online research. It also provides finding aids, guides, and research tools that can prepare you for a visit to either its Washington, D.C., facility or one of its thirteen regional facilities or for requesting records from NARA. URL: www.nara.gov/genealogy.

RootsWeb and Ancestry.com. This Web site provides a guide and interactive lessons for tracing your family tree as well as numerous free search engines and databases. URL: www.rootsweb.com.

FamilySearch. This is the genealogy Web site that the Church of Jesus Christ of Latter-Day Saints (also known as the Mormon Church) maintains. It is one of the largest collections of genealogy data in the world. URL: www.familysearch.com.

Genealogy.com. This Web site offers online genealogy courses as well as an extensive database and guides for researching your family tree. URL: www.genealogy.com.

GRANDCHILDPROOF YOUR HOME

How long has it been since you've had a toddler roaming your home? For many of us it's been a long time since we had to worry about cleaning products under the sink and whether the lid was down on the toilet. When we got the last child out of braces and through college, we bought the glass coffee table we always wanted and decorated the living areas with fragile keepsakes and knickknacks that just weren't practical during the child-raising years.

But now we have grandchildren. And we would all do well to remember that annually 4.5 million children are injured at home—2 million seriously enough to require medical attention—and Nana's house may contain as many potential dangers as their own homes do. Keeping a close eye on your grandchildren as well as taking simple preventive measures will keep your little ones from harm.

Here are some room-by-room tips for making every room as child-safe as possible:

Kitchen
- Install cabinet locks on low cabinets and drawers that contain sharp knives and potentially toxic cleaning products.

- Place kitchen appliances away from the edges of counters. Make sure electrical appliance cords aren't dangling from countertops.

- Keep toddlers away from the stove at all times. Mark off a zone that they know is not safe to enter.

- If stove knobs are within a child's reach, use protective covers to prevent the child from turning them on.

- When cooking, turn pot handles toward the back of the stove and use the back burners whenever possible.

- Keep counters clear of clutter.

- Place a pot or pan over a hot burner until it has cooled down.

- Keep high chairs, chairs, and step stools away from counters and the stove.

- Store cookies and treats your grandchildren might reach for far away from the stove area.

- Keep the kids out of the kitchen when you are frying.

- If possible, stow trash and recyclables in a locked cabinet or closet.

- Keep plastic bags, plastic wrap, and foil out of reach. Tie plastic bags in knots before storing or recycling them.

- Use place mats instead of a tablecloth so that your grandchild cannot pull the contents of the table down on top of himself or herself.

- Set the water heater to 120 degrees or cooler to prevent scalding from the kitchen faucet.

- Load silverware into the dishwasher with the handles facing up.

- Remove small magnets—potential choking hazards—from the fridge.

- Never hold a hot beverage while carrying your grand-child, no matter how careful you plan to be.

- Clean up broken glass slivers with a damp, disposable cloth and then vacuum. Mop thoroughly before letting your grandchildren back into the kitchen.

- Keep a working fire extinguisher handy.

A second honeymoon is a terrific idea—a chance for the two of you to spend some time alone, away from the numbing grind of your daily domestic routine, with nothing to distract you from days of pleasure and nights of passion except possibly a phone call from your mother asking if there is a particular pediatric surgeon you generally go to, or should she just pick one on her own.
                                                —Dave Barry

Bathroom

- Make sure electrical appliances such as blow-dryers are unplugged, away from water, and out of a child's reach.

- Store hazardous items such as razors, scissors, and medicines out of a child's reach, preferably in a locked cabinet.

- Make sure all medications have childproof lids.

- Keep the toilet seat down and the door to the bathroom closed or gated. Or buy hinged toilet lid locks that clamp to the lip of the bowl.

- Set the water heater to 120 degrees or cooler to prevent scalding from the bathroom sink and tub.

- Place a nonskid mat or decals in the bathtub.

- Use a large nonskid rug on the bathroom floor.

- Supervise your grandchildren's baths; don't use bath seats, which can tip.

- Test the bathwater before putting your grandchild in the tub.

- Toss a small hand towel over the top of a bathroom door when your grandchild is using the rest room so that it won't close completely. This way, little ones are less likely to lock themselves in.

Living Areas and Bedrooms

- Secure unstable furniture, such as bookshelves, entertainment centers, and dressers, that could topple if a child pulls on them.

- Install cushioned corners on the sharp corners of tables and other furniture with pointed edges.

- Move the TV, VCR, and stereo out of reach.

- Run electrical cords along baseboards, securing them to the floor when possible. Bind up any extra cord. Check regularly to make sure the cords are not frayed or overloaded.

- Install short cords on phones or secure the cords up high out of reach. Better still, use cordless phones. This way you eliminate the choking hazard and make yourself mobile, which means you never have to leave young grandkids unattended to answer the phone.

- Shorten long cords for blinds or draperies. Wrap them around wall brackets, wind them up, and tie the cords with a short string or buy a cord wrap.

- Set up safety gates at the bottoms and tops of staircases to protect small children.

- Position your grandchild's crib or bed away from windows, drapery, and electrical cords. Put nightlights at least three feet away from bedding and draperies to prevent fires.

- Keep pocket change and jewelry off the top of the dresser and out of reach.

- Light hallways and staircases to prevent falls.

- If you have older grandchildren whose toys have a lot of small pieces, buy organizing boxes with lids that close tightly.

- Use plastic outlet covers to prevent electrical shocks.

- Install a screen or locked-glass enclosure on your fireplace. Remove irons and tools. Install screens around radiators, wood-burning stoves, and kerosene heaters.

- Cover fireplace hearths with protective cushioning.

- Install smoke detectors on the ceiling outside sleeping or napping areas. Test the alarm monthly and replace the batteries twice a year.

- Keep a list of emergency numbers (fire, police, pediatrician, poison control) by the phone.

BE PREPARED

When you're in charge of a grandchild, make sure these emergency numbers are beside the telephone:

Baby's doctor

Poison-control center

Emergency medical and ambulance services

Fire department

In most areas 911 is the emergency help number, but it's best to confirm this in the area where you live.

Throughout the House

- Conduct a room-by-room inventory of potential dangers. If you have younger grandchildren, get down on all fours and view each room from their eye level. Make sure all potentially harmful items—cleaning products, perfumes, shoe polish, hair products, makeup, vitamins, mouthwash, medicine, alcoholic beverages, cigarettes, matches, and lighters—are out of a child's reach.

- Keep potted houseplants in inaccessible locations; some are poisonous.

- Put childproof covers on all electrical sockets.

- Use childproof window latches.

- Secure radiator covers and floor vents so that a child cannot pull them off.

- Affix decals at a child's eye level to glass doors or windows that extend down to the floor.

- Put slip-proof guards on uncarpeted stairs.

- Use nonslip carpet tape or sticky matting under area rugs to told them in place.

- Use safety gates on rooms without doors to keep children from wandering into dangerous areas.

- Install gates at the top and bottom of stairs. Don't use a tension-mounted gate at the top of the stairs. If a child leans on it, it could become dislodged.

- Put covers on doorknobs to rooms you don't want a child to enter. Or install hook-and-eye latches to keep doors closed.

- Make sure you can unlock any door inside your home from the outside in case a child locks himself or herself in a room.

- Set chairs and tables by walls, not windows.

- Consider installing plastic guards along the hinge side of frequently used interior doors to prevent pinched fingers.

- To prevent choking, remove plastic end caps on doorstops or replace the stops with a one-piece design.

- Lock the doors of rooms grandchildren shouldn't be in by themselves.

- Attach bells on exit doors to warn you if a child opens one.

- Don't place furniture so that a child is able to climb to a window or ledge.

GUNS IN THE HOME

If you have a gun in your home, it should be locked up where a child cannot get to it—ever! The American Academy of Pediatrics (AAP) says that the best way to prevent gun-related injuries and deaths is to remove guns from homes. However, if you or husband hunts, works in law enforcement or another profession in which guns are required, or wants a gun for protection, be aware that *any* gun can be deadly dangerous if a child finds it. Lock it up!

Outdoor Safety

- Make sure any raised porch or deck has a railing and that the railing isn't wide enough for a child to climb through. If it is, cover the railing with Plexiglas, strong mesh, or a lattice. Do the same thing for fences surrounding your property.

- Keep patio furniture away from the railings so that a child cannot climb on them and fall over.

- Check wooden decks regularly for splinters.

- Install a latch on the door leading to the balcony or yard.

- Install a hook and eye on the outside of the gate to the yard so that you can reach it but your grandchild can't.

- Regularly check swings and other play equipment for rust, loose screws, splintering wood, and sharp edges.

- Make sure children's play equipment is anchored securely before use. Test it yourself to detect potentially unsafe structures.

- Put covers on swing chains to avoid caught fingers and torn clothes.

- Put wood chips, sand, or mulch under the swing set or play area. The deeper the fill goes, the safer your grandchild will be in case of a fall. Make sure the fill

extends far enough that if your grandchild is pro-
pelled from a swing, he or she will land on a softer
surface.

- Never take a child for a ride on a garden tractor or
  riding mower.

- Do not mow the lawn with a child nearby. The blade
  often kicks up sharp objects.

- Return gardening equipment to a locked shed or an
  inaccessible part of the garage immediately after
  its use.

- If the yard is not fenced off from the street, establish a
  safety zone along the front yard that your grandchild
  knows to stay inside. Buy orange safety cones and
  teach your grandchild not to go past them.

- Keep the play area clean of pet droppings. Keep
  cats out of the sandbox by covering it when it is not
  in use.

- Coil and return the garden hose to its hanger when it
  is not in use.

- String clotheslines out of a grandchild's reach.

- Make sure wooden fences have rounded, well-sanded
  posts. Make sure that a chain-link fence has no barbs
  sticking up.

- Teach your grandchild to stay away from the barbecue
  grill.

- Get rid of highly poisonous or toxic plants in the
  back or front yard. Call the local poison-control center for a list of dangerous plants in your area.

- After a rainy period, remove any mushrooms or toadstools since they could be poisonous.

- Store ladders out of reach or secure them to the wall horizontally so that they will not tempt your grandchild to climb.

- Keep the car locked to prevent your grandchild from climbing inside and activating the garage door opener or knocking the car out of gear.

For more information about child safety and other issues vital to grandparents, visit the Children, Youth and Families Education and Research Network at www.cpsc.gov.

WHAT MAKES A GRANDPARENT GRAND?

I have dedicated this book to a dear friend and mentor whom I miss greatly. She understood that her children and grandchildren were a priceless gift and that she was invaluable to them. But just because she had five children and thirteen grandchildren on whom she showered love, attention, concern, and prayers, don't conjure up a picture of a grandmotherly type sitting on the front porch in her rocking chair, shelling peas. Maybe she sat down in a rocker after she briskly walked three miles or played two sets of tennis, and maybe you'd find her shelling peas late one night preparing for a big family picnic in her backyard. But for a correct picture of this incredible mom and grandmom, envision a sharp, savvy, in-shape, energetic sixty-two-year-old who looked and acted about ten years younger than her age. That's my idea of a grandmother.

Throughout this chapter we've explored the myriad ways we can be helpful, affectionate, vital grandparents. With all our education, experience, and know-how, perhaps the best thing we can give our grandchildren is plain old enthusiasm. Children sense when they are enjoyed or endured. If they feel and hear how glad you are to see them at each visit (whether it's in person or by phone or computer), they will feel special, celebrated, and worthwhile. What better building blocks for life?

Whether you are like my vibrant mentor or are more of a warm-lap-and-cookies grandparent, you play an enormous role in your grandchildren's development. Feel free to express every glad feeling you have to them—and they will return the favor.

8

Who Will Nurture
the Nurturer?

You will soon break the bow if you keep it always stretched.

—Phaedrus

If you've made it this far into the book, you and I probably have something very important in common: We want to be great mothers for a lifetime. We understand the far-reaching influence we have on those whose lives we touch. It is part of the fabric from which we're cut to care for, nurture, and sacrifice for the good of those we love.

My mind is overtaxed. Brave and courageous as I am, I feel the creeping on of that inevitable thing, a breakdown, if I cannot get some immediate relief. I need somebody to come and get me.

—Mary McLeod Bethune

Sacrifice may be the word with which we identify the most. A friend of mine put it like this: "When I was growing up, when the platter of fried chicken was passed around, my mother always chose the wing or the back. She said those were her favorite pieces, but I knew better. She just wanted her kids to have the best parts."

"Now that I'm a mother," she continued, "I understand firsthand the sense of fulfillment that comes from giving things up for or to your kids. I do it for mine, and when we're all together for a family occasion, I notice that my mother *still* leaves the best pieces of chicken for us and the grandkids. You never stop being a mother."

This is good and bad news. Mothering is a wonder-filled, satisfying, and challenging job—for a lifetime. I wouldn't give it up for anything. But the bad news is that typically mothers suffer from neglect. It's true: The caregiver receives the least care.

A NEED UNMET

One of my favorite parts of my work is traveling around the country and meeting thousands of women who attend my seminars. I love listening to their stories and offering advice about the problems and issues with which they are dealing. There's one complaint I hear again and again from coast to coast and border to border: Women are so busy caring for everyone else's needs, they don't have time to care for themselves. They're drained, sucked dry of emotional, physical, and spiritual energy. They know they can't just stop caring for their children and fulfilling the responsibilities of running a home, but they wonder if they'll make it.

Sound familiar? Yes, when our kids were young their constant demands were exhausting. Now our kids are grown, but they still need us, although in different ways; in addition, many of us also are caring for aging parents. At any age, unless Mom the nourisher nourishes herself, she won't have the emotional, physical, and spiritual stamina it takes now to be pulled from both ends: parenting older kids as well as parents.

When we're this overwhelmed, we often find little pleasure in life. We have no buffer between us and relentless everyday pressures. Something's got to give, and it's usually us.

Researchers strongly agree on two basic principles: first, that man has limited capacity; and second, that overloading the system leads to serious breakdown of performance.
—Alvin Toffler

The buffer we all need comes from *self-care.* When we take time to rejuvenate, it pays off in many ways, including being a better mom, grandmom, wife, daughter, and friend. When we don't, that also pays off in many ways. One woman commented, "When I forget my own needs, I become angry at every demand on my time, from my husband to my mother to my children and grandchildren, to coworkers and friends—even the dog!" To fail to invest in our own value through self-care is to put not only ourselves but also the people we care about at risk. After all, an exhausted and deflated mom, wife, or daughter is no good to anyone.

TEN REASONS WOMEN DON'T TAKE CARE OF THEMSELVES

1. *Circumstances.* We live under the tyranny of the urgent: Whatever or whoever is screaming the loudest gets the attention; something or someone is always making noise. One friend calls this "managing by fire": She deals with whatever is creating the most smoke at any given moment. "My mother wants me to help her clean out her basement, my daughter

needs me to keep her baby, my husband wants to have his sales team over for dinner, my best friend is having a hysterectomy and needs me to take her to and from the hospital and help with postop care, my dog's in heat. Everything is urgent—at least it seems that way—except caring for myself."

2. *Others' expectations.* We're all prone to succumb to the agendas of others. When was the last time you said yes to a request simply because some domineering person—perhaps a cranky elderly parent or a desperate-sounding daughter—asked it of you?

I don't know the key to success, but the key to failure is trying to please everybody.
—Bill Cosby

---

3. *Natural boundaries.* We simply can't do all there is to do with the limited number of hours and amount of energy we have each day. We must make choices accordingly. Back to my friend in reason 1. Can she clean out her mother's basement later, even next week? Can her daughter find someone else to babysit? Can the dinner party wait until her friend recovers? Until someone finds a way to add another hour or two to each day, the answer to these questions should be yes. As for the question, "Will you let a day go by without carving out some time to care for you?" the answer should be no.

4. *Lack of focus.* If we don't examine our situation once in a while, we're never sure what we want or need to be doing because we haven't stopped long enough to

figure it out. Rethinking our priorities and focus at this stage in life is important. Evaluation is sometimes painful, but it's the first step in getting one's life in focus. Envisioning is next—deciding where we want to go in the second half of life and who we want to be. Taking some actions—however small—to move in the direction we want to go is where change begins.

Everything becomes different when we choose to take control rather than be controlled. We experience a new sense of freedom, growth, and energy.
—Dr. Eric Allenbaugh

---

5. *Love of comfort.* It's been said that the definition of insanity is doing the same things over and over and expecting things to change. We all tend to avoid change if possible. As we get older, we want fewer surprises and a minimum of inconvenience, and so we avoid the new in favor of the familiar—even though the familiar may be substandard. Consequently, we miss out on the good change often brings.

Change is not made without inconvenience, even from worse to better.
—Samuel Johnson

---

6. *Not enough time.* Between family, friends, work, and more, finding time for ourselves seems like an elusive, if not impossible, task. But in reality we do have the time; it's a matter of what we choose to spend it

on. We will never "find" time for anything. If we
want time, we must make it.

---

*Time is the coin of your life. It is the only coin you
have, and only you can determine how it will be spent.
Be careful lest you let other people spend it for you.*
—Carl Sandburg

---

7. *Fear of failure or rejection.* Safety has a friendly face,
but it's deceptive. Sometimes the kindest and best
thing we can do for ourselves and those we love is
take a risk. Maybe you feel you've earned the acceptance of your son and daughter-in-law through your
willingness to have them for dinner on Sunday
night. Now you fear telling them you want to get to
bed early on Sunday night because you're starting a
new job. Since things are going smoothly, you don't
want to rock the boat. The problem is that if you
never think of what's best when it comes to caring
for yourself, your boat will sink.

8. *Misunderstanding the process.* Like any habit or
change in lifestyle, making self-care a priority is not
an overnight occurrence. Making small changes every
day, such as giving yourself time to read a favorite
book, buying yourself a bunch of tulips, or keeping a
journal of your thoughts and prayers, eventually can
make a really big difference in one's life.

9. *Lack of connection with the big picture.* When our
eyes are fixed on getting through just this hour or
this day, there's no way we can begin to plan for next
week, much less next month or year. As the old

saying goes, we can't see the forest for the trees, and we won't give ourselves the gift of getting away for a while to renew our perspective on life.

10. *Pride.* Sometimes we are simply unwilling to admit our need for change or help. If we haven't made self-care a priority, chances are, we're using something—alcohol, drugs, overeating—to provide at least a temporary escape from reality. But temporary is the operative word here. If we are trying to escape in an unhealthy way, we only make the problem worse.

We all probably can identify with one or more of those reasons, but I believe there is one all-important underlying excuse for why we neglect ourselves: *We don't see ourselves as worthy of care.*

Too many people overvalue what they are not and undervalue what they are.

—Malcolm Forbes

Let me ask you a question: If I drove up today and handed you the keys to a brand-new sports car—free of charge—would you keep it maintained, washed, and filled with gas? I think you would. If I gave you a thoroughbred horse as a present, would you make sure it was fed, brushed, and exercised? Probably so. Why? We take care of the things we deem valuable. It would be an eye-opening experience for many of us if we took a good hard look at what we really perceive as worthy of attention.

A woman I met recently breeds show dogs. She cares so much for her dogs that she has a special room in the house just for them. She feeds them a very expensive kind of dog food. When they travel to dog shows, they ride in a plush, custom-decorated trailer. Hearing her story helped me think about the extremes to which people go to care for the things they value. If we don't value ourselves, it's doubtful that we'll take care of ourselves. And if we don't take care of ourselves, it's a sure bet: We will put not only ourselves but also those we care for at risk.

Love your neighbor as yourself, we're told. Maybe before I can love my neighbor very effectively, I have to love me—not in the sense of a blind passion but in the sense of looking after, of wishing well, of forgiving when necessary, of being my own friend.

—Frederick Buechner

Although putting your own needs last may seem the right or noble thing to do, the truth is that when you don't take care of yourself, you're not doing yourself, your spouse, your children, or anyone else in your care any favors.

Friendship with oneself is all-important because without it one cannot be friends with anyone else in the world.

—Eleanor Roosevelt

Love—or the lack of it—forms the foundation of how we see ourselves. When we love people, we're eager and willing to spend time and energy taking care of them, meeting their needs, and watching them flourish. We must begin to see ourselves as people worth loving and treat ourselves with as much loving kindness as we lavish on others.

Care begets itself. When you honor your own needs and desires, you naturally honor those of others as well. The way we treat ourselves inevitably affects the way we treat others. Taking care of yourself is a win/win situation.

DO YOU SEE YOURSELF AS VALUABLE AND WORTHY OF CARE?

Answering these questions will give you a good idea about the areas you need to invest in to practice better self-care.

- Do you get sufficient rest?

- Do you eat nutritious foods?

- Do you get regular physicals?

- Do you take vitamin supplements?

- Do you purposefully do things you enjoy to unwind: take bubble baths, pursue hobbies, get together with friends, put on soothing music?

- Do you give yourself facials and take care of your skin with good products?

- Do you make it a point to spend time with stimulating, upbeat people?

- Do you exercise regularly?

- Do you read books?

- Are you proactively learning things you want to know more about?

- Do you allow yourself to pursue new hobbies and interests?

- Do you allow yourself to take mini-midweek retreats, such as to a museum or a park?

- Do you collect ideas and quotes that stimulate your thinking or enhance your life?

- Do you allow yourself to develop your talent and interest in music?

- Do you attend services or classes that stimulate your spiritual growth and understanding?

- Do you buy or cut fresh flowers to enjoy at your home or on your desk at the office?

- Do you make some quiet time to think about where you are in life, about your goals and aspirations?

- Do you keep a journal of your thoughts and prayers?

- Do you keep a dream file of brochures and articles about faraway places you'd like to visit?

- Do you buy or check out books on tape or CDs from a bookstore or public library for listening and learning in the car?

- Do you splurge a little every now and then by doing or buying something special for yourself?

- Do you allow yourself to get a massage every so often?

- Do you allow yourself to learn new things, maybe smocking, photography, or flower arranging?

- Do you reward yourself with something enjoyable when you've finished a big chore or project?

- Do you allow yourself to join a group you're interested in, such as a drama team, an arts and crafts club, a tennis league, or a church choir?

- Do you spend time regularly with close, affirming friends?

You probably have identified several areas that need attention. Don't make the mistake of trying to fix everything at once. Tackle one area this week: Begin building a new habit of self-nurturance. Mother yourself. And watch the results begin to set you free.

IT'S HOW YOU REACT THAT COUNTS

When we feel stretched, we have three possible responses:

1. We can blame others. When I realize I'm exhausted beyond reason, I can blame my husband: "If you had remembered to pick up the dry cleaning, I'd have had time to get to the grocery store."

2. We can beat up on ourselves. "If I had just been better organized, I could have handled both my errands and mother's. I'm so useless, I can't even discipline myself."

The art of being wise is the art of knowing what to overlook.
                                                    —William James

---

3. We can make the best of the situation. Seeing a situation for what it is without using our built-in situation enlarger to blow it out of proportion is an art. After a few minutes of self-abuse I realize that nobody is dead or hurt. Nothing crucial to life has been lost. So no one made it to the grocery store; we can have takeout tonight and shop tomorrow. My husband isn't a bad person for forgetting; nor am I. What's the big deal? So I

didn't get all my errands run. That's not the end of the world. (Sometimes we have to go through the first two responses to get to the third.)

STOP THE MADNESS! STRATEGIES FOR A SANER LIFE

Perhaps you've gone so long without "you time" that burnout has taken over. You feel hopeless and helpless about the state of things. Please believe me, you can start again. When burnout threatens, it's time to simplify. As you begin managing your life so that you can enjoy it more, burnout will turn into enthusiasm. Here's a four-step plan to get you going.

1. Track Your Time

The path to serenity begins with getting a handle on what's filling up your days. It's not unusual to get to the end of a week and wonder where the time went. Too many commitments, seemingly urgent circumstances, and an unrealistic to-do list as well as a lack of discipline can contribute to robbing us of precious peaceful hours.

To help you discover where your time is going, keep a log of how you spend your time for the next three days. This may seem like a nuisance, but it's important. Include the following:

	Day1	Day2	Day3
Regular work hours			
Getting ready for the day			
Helping Mom or Dad			
Helping adult children			
Baby-sitting grandkids			

	Day1	Day2	Day3
Shopping			
Preparing and eating meals			
Attending meetings			
Volunteering			
Talking on the phone			
Watching television			
Browsing the Internet			
Reading and answering e-mails			
Cleaning house			
Doing laundry for your family and parents			
Running errands for your family and parents			
Backtracking			
Exercising			
Working on projects or hobbies			
Reading			
Personal care (manicure, facial, haircut)			
Searching for misplaced items			
Solving other people's problems			
Dealing with financial issues			
Doing something just for you or just for fun			
Relaxing or doing nothing			
Praying or meditating			
Getting ready for bed			
Sleeping			

You may find that you are committing a lot of time to too many nonpriority items or doing things for other people that they can do for themselves. You also may discover that you're spending dangerously little time on things that refresh you.

2. Evaluate Your Choices

Now that you can see on paper where your time is going, you can evaluate your choices and start looking for ways to cut back—*things not to do*—so that you can create a healthier, saner lifestyle.

Use the following questions to help you get started:

- What are you doing that could be left undone? Do you really have to vacuum the house more than twice a week? Can you help your daughter make curtains after the holidays instead of now?

There are two ways of meeting difficulties: You alter the difficulties, or you alter yourself to meet them.
—Phyllis Bottome

- What are you doing that someone else could do? Can someone else help your son complete his tax forms? Do you really have to pick up other family members' clutter? Do you have a sibling who could help you pay for someone to clean your parents' house?

- How are you allowing other people to interrupt your day and determine your schedule? Do you have to answer the phone every time it rings? Do you have to check your e-mail every time you hear the "you've got mail" chime?

- Are there any activities to which you transport your parents that they really don't enjoy and could do without?

- Are you committed to volunteer projects just because you couldn't refuse the person who recruited you?

- Are you keeping the grandkids an inordinate amount of time to make sure your daughter has time for herself but now have little personal time for yourself?

Every now and then go away, have a little relaxation, for when you come back to your work your judgment will be surer; since to remain constantly at work will cause you to lose power of judgment. . . . Go some distance away, because the work appears smaller, and more of it can be taken in at a glance, and a lack or harmony or proportion is more readily seen.

—Leonardo DaVinci

- Do you shop and run errands when everyone else is doing the same thing?

- Do you spend a lot of time searching for misplaced items or sifting through piles of papers?

- Do you take enough time to do things that renew your body, soul, and mind?

- What things are you doing that are not top priority and important to you?

3. Make a Not-to-Do List.

After you evaluate your choices and begin to see the time robbers in your life, make a different kind of list: things you've decided *not* to do. Here are some examples:

- *Don't let other people set your standards.* Just because your mother has come to live at your house, don't do housework a certain way simply because that's the way she always did it and she checks for dust every day.

- *Don't be everyone else's maid.* Don't do things for family members they could do for themselves. If a man can learn how to program a VCR so that he won't miss game four of the World Series, he can start the washing machine. If an elderly woman can watch the soaps, she can fold some laundry while she's sitting there.

- *Don't let other people interrupt your day.* Let voice mail or an answering machine take your calls. Call people back when it's convenient for you. If your daughter calls just to get caught up, arrange to talk while you're doing something else—such as preparing dinner—or set up a regular appointment to chat.

- *Don't overschedule yourself.* Honestly think about why you are involved in so many extra activities. Do you have to teach Sunday school *and* serve on the missions committee? Do you have to attend every game your grandchildren play, or could you limit yourself to one or two a week?

The time to relax is when you don't have time for it.
—Sydney J. Harris

- *Don't let other people determine what's most important.* You must decide what you and your family value. Establishing priorities will help you focus your time and energy and help you know when to say yes and when to say no. For example, if you've decided it's a priority to take a water aerobics class and then eat lunch with friends once a week, treat that time as you would a doctor's appointment: something you can't cancel or delay.

We cannot be a source of strength unless we nurture our own strength.
—M. Scott Peck

- *Don't neglect yourself.* As you think about the things you are not going to do and begin scratching items off your to-do list, don't eliminate things that nourish you. As a matter of fact, in the slots of time you create it's a good idea to add some things that make your health and serenity a priority. Give yourself permission to sit outside and read a book. Make an appointment for a pedicure. Carve out a block of time for exercise.

4. Know Your No-Matter-Whats.

Be committed to your personal life support system. Know your no-matter-whats: the habits and actions in your life that take precedence no matter who is pushing you to do things differently. These are the things you don't skip, and they should include methods of self-care.

MY OWN NO-MATTER-WHATS— AND YOURS

We all have seasons in our lives that are more difficult and draining than others. Stress comes in many forms: physical issues, a parent moving in with us, a twenty-one-year-old who can't seem to get her feet planted on solid ground, the fact that we're now parenting grandchildren, a financial strain that has left us weary and frightened. Whatever the causes, each of us has to decide that no matter what's going on in life, these are the things we do regularly to nurture ourselves.

I learned this lesson early in life when my children were in their busiest years. I took care of everyone else but didn't manage myself and ended up in the hospital. I don't want to go there again, and so ever since that time I've been religious about my no-matter-whats. For me this means that no matter what life brings:

> I will seek to care for my body wisely, taking vitamins, eating wisely, exercising regularly, and drinking lots of water.
>
> I will care for my mind by learning and reading.
>
> I will nourish my spirit through Bible study and prayer.

I asked a number of women to share with me their no-matter-whats. As you read theirs, be thinking of your own. No matter what I will:

> Do something every day that makes me happy.
>
> Soak in my bathtub and read part of a novel. (I have a waterproof bath pillow that attaches to the tub with suction cups and a bathtub shelf I place across the tub. It's perfect for holding a book out of the water.)
>
> Get dressed. Staying in my robe all day makes me depressed.
>
> Get my nails done.
>
> Do my Bible study. It feeds my spirit.
>
> Take myself to my favorite coffee shop. It has large, comfortable chairs where I sit, sip coffee, and peruse my

ever-accumulating stack of catalogs. I don't take my cell phone with me. This is my time.

Go to my exercise class.

Get regular facials.

Write in my journal.

Walk my dogs.

Take a short nap. (When I read that Albert Einstein and Thomas Edison took catnaps in the middle of the day so that they could better work on their experiments, I decided to give myself the freedom to do the same thing.)

Play tennis.

In all our lives, some days are frenetic, but every day we all have at least a few minutes to spend caring for ourselves.

WHO ARE YOU?

Perhaps you've neglected yourself for so long that you have forgotten what you like to do or who you want to be. If you're having trouble painting even a general picture of what your no-matter-whats are, try the following exercises. You don't need to limit yourself to three answers for each question, but I've found that the first three things that come immediately to mind often are the heart's secret desires.

- Write down three things you used to enjoy doing and would like to do again. Write down three things you would like to try at least once to see if you like them.

  _____

  _____

  _____

- Write down three things you know would be good for your body.

  _____

  _____

  _____

- Write down three things you'd like to change about your appearance.

  _____

  _____

  _____

- Write down three habits you'd like to lose.

  _____

  _____

  _____

- Write down three habits you'd like to incorporate into your life.

  _____

  _____

  _____

- Write down the titles of three movies you would like to see.

  _____

  _____

  _____

- Write down three books or magazines you would like to read.

  _____

  _____

  _____

- Write down three things you feel would nourish you spiritually.

  _____

  _____

  _____

- Write down the names of three friends you'd like to see more often.

  _____

  _____

  _____

- Write down three hobbies that sound like fun.

  _____

  _____

  _____

- Write down three skills you would like to learn.

  _____

  _____

  _____

- Write down three places where you would like to go on vacation.

  _____

  _____

  _____

Once you've done all this, go back over your list. Who is the person who would like to do these things? How does she spend her time? What does she look like? Would you like to know her better? Are you beginning to see her?

Now, what does that woman consider essential activities? Start your list!

YOU'RE NOT THE QUEEN OF EVERYTHING

Isn't that great? Admit you're human, not superhuman. You can't be responsible for the whole world. You can't do everything that needs to be done, regardless of its value, and you won't meet everyone's expectations. That's reality, and that's freedom.

Realize that every sane person has to live by priorities in relationships, including your relationship with yourself. And since every day is a new one with fresh opportunities, challenges, and family needs and demands, managing this part of life does not have an easy formula. It is a constant process. When you blow it and find yourself depleted, give yourself the freedom and time needed to recover—and determine to make a better choice next time.

When you learn to say yes to yourself and no to unnecessary demands on your time, you'll discover newfound energy for accomplishing what's important. You'll have less stress and more peace of mind. It's the ultimate cure for impending madness as well as the ultimate gift you can give yourself and those around you.

Go ahead—take a drumstick or a breast. It's your chicken too!

9
What Family Is All About

Commitment, hard work, and perseverance are indeed essential elements in making a modern family succeed, but, today no less than yesterday or the day before, the rewards are matchless, taking the form of love, deep friendship, tenderness, mutuality, the refinement of the soul—and much laughter to boot.

—William Bennett

*O*ur family enjoys listening to Garrison Keillor's stories about Lake Wobegon, where all the women are strong, the men are good-looking, and the children are above average. I travel to many Lake Wobegon–like places—and live in one as well—where there are a lot of beautiful people who live in beautiful homes, drive beautiful cars, and have beautiful children. These people look so good on the outside, it's tempting to think there is such a thing as a perfect family—that mine is just not one of them. God must have skipped us when he was making five-star families.

But deep down I know that's not true. None of us has a perfect or pain-free family. The storms of life hit rich and poor, educated and uneducated, young and old alike. None of us knows what tomorrow will bring in the form of aches and pains, broken bones, infections, disease, auto accidents, bankruptcy, divorce, disappointment, betrayal, neglect, abuse, terrorist attacks, or death. I doubt there are any among us who could say they do not experience pain to some degree daily.

Great and small suffer the same mishaps.
—Blaise Pascal

What separates healthy families from unhealthy families is not whether we have problems—because all families do—but how we handle them. Healthy families understand that home is a place to rest where they can find a shoulder to lean on, a listening ear, a helping hand, a shelter in times of need. Healthy families cherish their bonds, and so they pay attention to anything that strains or threatens their relationships. They provide on-site training for growing human beings to know how to care for a wide variety of emotional and physical pains because each person has received loving care and has watched it being given to others.

Life becomes harder for us when we live for others, but it also becomes richer and happier.
—Albert Schweitzer

When we find ourselves in the middle of difficult times, we know that times like these are a part of the whole of life. They are not unimportant disruptions we can shove aside or try to deny so that they can get back to "normal." We know this is normal life. And being there for each other in times of trouble and pain, as well as times of joy and celebration, is what it's all about.

There are four ways a healthy family helps its members prepare for and engage in life:

1. *It provides emotional stability.* Every human being
   has a need to belong. As painful as relationships
   may be for some of us, we long for intimacy: to
   know and be known by someone else. This is essential for emotional development and security. The
   family is the place that shelters us from the stresses
   and demands of life—one place where we're safe,
   where we can be close to other people and receive
   their love and acceptance simply because we're family.
   It doesn't matter what we look like, what we do,
   how smart we are, or how much money we make.
   When a family provides this kind of emotional
   strength, every member has a stable platform from
   which to engage a shaky world and courageously
   face the crises of life.

---

*The race of mankind would perish did they cease to
aid each other. We cannot exist without mutual help.*
                                              —Sir Walter Scott

---

A few years ago I went through a very difficult
passage. People I had trusted let me down. My personal code of ethics was tested as individuals tried to
persuade me to agree to business decisions and part-
nerships I believed were morally wrong. A legal battle
ensued that left me emotionally limp and financially
drained. I felt like a failure. There were days I wondered if I could go on. But I believe I not only made
it through but came through stronger and wiser
because I had parents who called to remind me how
much they love and believe in me, a husband who
loves and cares for me and reminds me every day

how much God loves me, and children who walked through the hard times with me, encouraging me with their words, e-mails, notes, and prayers. Being reminded that there are people who know me—warts and all—and still love and believe in me was powerful therapy.

Love is the basic need of human nature, for without it, life is disrupted emotionally, mentally, spiritually and physically.

—Dr. Karl Menninger

---

2. *It provides economic viability.* Throughout history we can see that the closer men and women lived to subsistence, the more they needed each other. It took everyone in a family working together for anyone to make it. Any force that threatened a family's stability also threatened its survival. Likewise, in early America large family units were key to survival on the frontier.

Today the economic forces that threaten the family are different. We don't all have to work together on the farm to make it. But we still can work and pull together even when we're thousands of miles apart, thanks to technology, helping each other survive and thrive. When a son is trying to get his business going, we can send him helpful information via the Internet. We can counsel him over the phone when he asks for advice about dealing with a difficult boss. When a daughter has a baby her last semester of medical school, we can fly in to help her with the house and the baby. Even now, as I am up all hours of the night finishing this book, my parents are calling to cheer me on, my husband is carving time out of his schedule to read and critique what I am writing, our boys who live in another city are checking in daily to encourage me, and our son who lives with us asks if he can help me out by running errands I don't have time to run. We are committed to working and pulling together for a lifetime, because we are family.

We are all in the same boat in a stormy sea, and we owe each other a terrible loyalty.
—G. K. Chesterton

---

3. *It provides cultural training.* Home base is where knowledge about life, values, traditions, and customs passes from grandparent to parent to child. Picture a relay race in which one generation hands over what it deems valuable: how it views the world, its definition of truth, and on what it bases those beliefs. Just as in a relay, sometimes the handoff is smooth, and other times someone drops the baton—but the relay continues no matter how the handoff goes.

   Whatever it is we hope to pass on to our children and grandchildren, we need to be intentional about it. If we aren't, other societal forces will answer their questions about their identity, parameters for right and wrong, and what's important in life—and we may not like the answers they provide. Escalating violence and killings by young adults in this country should cause us, the parents, to check the location of our baton.

4. *It provides relational training.* Whether we treat others with respect and dignity or with disregard and indifference is largely a matter of how we have learned to relate to our own family members. How we settle conflicts; how we express love and affection, anger and frustration to each other; whether we respect authority figures—all these things we glean in the context of the family.

History teaches us that there is no substitute for the family if we are to have a society that stands for human beings at their best.

—Ray Lyman Wilbur

We learn to value and treat others by what we see modeled in our family. One of Grimm's fairy tales provides a poignant illustration. As the story goes, a mother, a father, their fourteen-year-old son, and their aging grandfather all lived together. The grandfather's hands were unsteady, and at mealtimes he often missed his mouth. Eventually they removed him from their table to eat in the corner, alone and in disgrace. After he dropped his bowl one day, they took away his utensils, leaving him to feed from a trough.

Soon afterward, the father found their son doing some woodworking in the shed. When the father asked the boy what he was doing, the son said, smiling up for approval, "I am making a trough to feed you and Mama out of when I get big."

Soon the old man was back at his place at the table, eating from a plate.

IN MY OPINION

Families today are so busy. It's not just my kids, but my grandkids and great-grandkids too. There's no time anymore to sit out on the porch or around the dinner table and tell stories. That's how you pass down your family history, family culture, and values to the next generation. I think we're seeing what happens in a society where that's not important—we have a lot of kids who don't have a family identity. But Hollywood producers have told them *their* stories with *their* values. We see the results of that.

—Myra, age 87

The most important single influence in the life of a person is another person . . . who is worthy of emulation.
—Paul D. Shafer

EXPANDING THE DEFINITION
OF FAMILY

Family is not a welcome idea for everyone. If abuse, desertion, or other forms of cruelty fractured your home life, the characteristics of a healthy family and the affection of blood relatives may seem like an alien concept to you. It doesn't have to be that way. You can redefine *family* to mean any people who are always glad to see you, who are your stable support in a shaky world, who offer a haven from life's hard times. And you can make a family wherever you go.

Perhaps you are part of a warm and dedicated group of parents and siblings. You probably know some cast-off folks who could use what you have. Consider the following ways some folks have redefined *family* for themselves and developed a new boundary to include those around them.

- A friend of mine who was adopted lost her mother and father when she was in college. The parents had no siblings, and so my friend didn't have any aunts or uncles, and she didn't know her biological family. Another family "adopted" her as their grown daughter, and she spends holidays and vacations with them.

- I have a number of single friends who have never married but have adopted babies in their forties. They are families in every sense of the word.

- My best friend is as close as a sister. Our families spend many holidays together, and we agreed to raise each other's children if something happened to one of us. We're not related by blood, but we are in every other way family.

- Another friend and her husband, whose kids are grown, have become foster parents.

- A young couple whose parents live out of the country have asked an older couple in their apartment complex to become their child's surrogate grandparents.

- Many families I know have encouraged their grown kids who live in a faraway city to create a community "family" there through a church or synagogue or with the families of friends.

THE PLACE WHERE WE LEARN WHO WE ARE

Writer and parent educator Jean Illsley Clark said volumes about the family: It's where we learn who we are and how to be that way. A long time ago my father did something small that had a big impact on the way I see myself. In my bid to be popular during my sophomore year in college, I had been sowing a lot of wild oats: staying out late partying and skipping a lot of classes. It wasn't long before my grades started to plummet along with my self-esteem. I wanted to drop out of school—and quickly—before they booted me out the door.

What families have in common the world around is that they are the place where people learn who they are and how to be that way.

—Jean Illsley Clarke

Dad, a no-nonsense business executive, took me to lunch. Rather than criticize me and predict my doom, he simply reminded me firmly but lovingly who I was. "Kathy, in our family we are not quitters," he said matter-of-factly. "When we fall down, we get back up."

He then told me the story of how his father left home when he was a young child. The burden of raising two boys during the Depression fell on his mother, who worked long hours as a seamstress. Daddy and his brother found odd jobs around town as they grew up, including one at his uncle's funeral home, where he had to spend hours alone at night with corpses in a big, old creaking house—which scared him half to death. He saved enough money to attend a nearby college and then joined the navy and helped fight the Japanese in the Pacific. All this by the time he was nineteen years old.

My father continued his story, all the while making a heartfelt point to me: Life is not always easy. In our family, when things get tough, we keep going. We do what we have to do. We are not quitters: "You're a bright young lady with a lot of potential. Now go back to college and do the best you can."

I returned to college and salvaged what grades I could. The next semester I made the dean's list.

We do not see things as they are. We see them as we are.
—the Talmud

My father had done a powerful thing: He had reminded me of who I was as a part of a larger family legacy of people who don't quit when things get tough. Although his own father had dropped the baton, my dad picked it up and handed it to me. My kids have heard that message from me again and again over the years. I want to keep passing along this family value.

We all can think of people whose parents and grandparents handed down a positive legacy. Their predecessors left footprints of integrity, kindness, generosity, philanthropy, service to humankind or one's country, the importance of education and continuing learning, faith in God, and the like.

My husband's father died twenty years ago. Although he didn't leave Bill a lot of money, he left a legacy of hard work and strong character. Bill's dad wasn't perfect, of course. No one is. But he taught Bill love and compassion toward mankind and a strong faith in God. When Bill was twenty-eight years old, his dad told him that every day, without fail, he prayed for fifty people, one of whom was Bill. What beautiful footprints he left in the sand of life for his son to follow. Every day Bill prays for numerous people.

This legacy passed down to Bill didn't start with his father. His dad was raised by his paternal grandparents after his mother had died in childbirth. Papa and Mama Peel were farmers and were people of deep faith, as those who live off the land often are. They were hardworking, praying folk who knew their well-being year after year rested in whether there was plenty of rain, a drought, or a flood on the Brazos River. As Bill's father told stories about his grandparents and his childhood on the farm, Bill learned that being a Peel is about hard work and faith, and it was something of which to be proud.

In contrast, we all can probably think of people we know whose parents or grandparents left a negative legacy that continues to plague them. Those relatives created a heritage of qualities such as dishonesty, irresponsibility, bitterness, and other destructive emotions. We cannot erase the footprints they have left, yet that legacy does not have to lead to further paths of destruction.

Many a family tree needs trimming.
                                        —Kin Hubbard

The movie *Catch Me if You Can* is a good example of this. It's the true story of sixteen-year-old Frank Abagnale, Jr., a young man who led the FBI on a chase across the United States and Europe as he assumed the identities of a high school teacher, an airline pilot, a physician, and an attorney before being caught, stealing several million dollars along the way. Where did Frank learn this outrageous behavior? According to the story, he learned it from his father. Fortunately, through the help of the FBI agent who tracked him down, today

Frank Abagnale has made a new identity for himself and has a legal job.

I have been greatly blessed by hearing the stories of many people who by their choices, their convictions, and their courage have overcome a negative legacy. They rejected the overwhelming pain of their pasts and embraced hope that they could still enjoy and contribute to life. And they changed the course of history in their families in bold and healthy ways.

One friend shared with me how she had to fight to overcome the ruinous legacy her mother left her: "I hate to say it, but no one was very sad when she died. She was a bitter, spiteful woman, and she made holidays and family occasions miserable for everyone." Despite the wounds of her past, this daughter today is a kind and gracious woman and a loyal, loving mother who organizes holiday festivities and special occasions in such a way that all who attend are blessed.

A man cannot leave a better legacy to the world than a well-educated family.

—Thomas Scott

Another friend, Joe, told me how his family did not value education or learning. He dropped out of high school at age sixteen and became a sanitation worker. Two years later he hurt his back lifting a garbage can and could no longer work in that position. Through the encouragement of his parish priest, he went to night school and got a GED. At age nineteen he was the first person in his family to receive a high school diploma. This experience, along with the encouragement of "Father John," as my friend calls him, whetted his appetite for learning. He enrolled in night classes at a local college and spent every hour he could, outside his nine-to-five job, studying and reading, which, I might add, were doubly hard for him as he is dyslexic.

In six years Joe graduated from college with an A average. Then his hunger to learn, the pride of having a college degree, and the continuing encouragement of Father John put him on the path to graduate school. Today he holds a doctorate from a prestigious university. Both of his sons have college degrees, and Joe continues to be an inspiration to others about the value of education and learning. He changed the legacy in his family and is leaving good footprints to follow.

WHAT ARE YOU PASSING DOWN TO YOUR CHILDREN AND GRANDCHILDREN?

The way our grandparents lived their lives affected our parents: their sense of identity, the values they embraced, and the way they raised us. The way we are living our lives is affecting members of our family today and will continue to touch them and their children when we're gone. Whether we realize it or not, ever since we laid eyes on our children in the delivery room, we have been teaching them—albeit unconsciously much of the time—who they are and how to be that way. We've been creating and living a legacy that will outlast us. We have taught and continue to teach our children and their children what we deem important in life: how we treat other human beings and the planet we live on, what spiritual truths are essential to life, our standards of right and wrong, and what we can do to make the world a better place. We may never have put any of this in writing, but we live it out every day.

The good news is that as the old adage says, "more is caught than taught"; this is also the bad news. Our kids and grandkids pick up from us what we really believe from our actions. If we don't back our words with action, they see it, absorb it, and probably will repeat it.

As Dr. Armand Nicholi of Harvard Medical School writes in his booklet *What Do We Know About Successful Families?*, "Our family experience is the most significant experience of our lives. . . . [It determines] our adult character structure, the inner picture we harbor of ourselves, how we feel about ourselves, how we perceive and feel about others, our concept of right and wrong—that is, the fundamental rules of human conduct that we call morality."

What you teach your son, you teach your son's son.
—the Talmud

If we want to influence in a positive way our children and grandchildren's character and pass to them a healthy legacy, three A's must characterize our words and actions.

First, our words and actions must be *affirmative.* Some parents and grandparents seem to be better at defining what they are against than what they are for. For example, we should be *for* healthy families, not just against forces that devalue or destroy the family. We should be *for* mutual respect of men, women, and children, not just against pornography. Every time we label something as wrong, we should describe or ask what would be right—what we can support in its stead. If we don't, we'll create a legacy of criticism and negativity. The truth of the matter is that there's always going to be something wrong with the world. Are we going to point our children and grandchildren toward what will make it right?

The way we communicate must be *attractive.* Perhaps this sounds like an odd question with an obvious answer, but do

your children and grandchildren know you love them unconditionally, that you're on their team? You may be thinking, "Of
course I love my kids and I'm on their team," but that wasn't
the question. Do your kids and grandkids *know* you love them
unconditionally and are on their team?

Good character, like good soup, is made at home.
—B. C. Forbes

One of the worst things we can do as parents or grandparents is to use our standards as a condition for our love and
approval. While we need to be honest about disagreeing with
their behavior or the values they embrace, our children and
grandchildren need to know that their value to us never
changes. No matter what their ages, they must sense that we
love them, seek to understand their feelings, and value them as
individuals. It's unlikely that they will accept our values if they
don't value their relationship with us.

---

*Example teaches better than precept. It is the best
modeler of the character of men and women. To set a
lofty example is the richest bequest a man can leave
behind him.*
—Samuel Smiles

Our lives must be *authentic*. We must do more than talk
about what we value and believe in; we must live those values
and beliefs. If we say we value honesty, our children and
grandchildren must observe our integrity. If we say we believe
in love and respect for others, they must see love and respect
for others in action. If we say we are Christian, or Jewish,

or Muslim, how do they see our faith making a difference in our lives?

A MORAL AND SPIRITUAL LEGACY

Now that your children and mine have reached that age of choice, it's a good time to evaluate what we've passed on so far. If we've tried to teach them, for example, integrity, a life-long love of learning, sensitivity to others, a strong work ethic, and our spiritual beliefs, what difference have our kids seen in our lives as a result of these qualities? Have we practiced honesty in our transactions with other people and with the government? Have we continued to be students, making lifelong learning a priority? Have we treated others with care and compassion? Have we been hard, steady workers? Have we let our religious beliefs affect our everyday decisions? In short, have we lived consistently what we say we believe, and when we've made mistakes—and there have been many, to be sure—have we admitted them and left no room for hypocrisy? In short, do our kids want what we have, or do they want to run the other way?

> *The religion of a child depends on what its mother and father are, and not on what they say.*
> —H. F. Amiel

Remember that whatever your mistakes of the past were, it's never too late to make changes, to say "I'm sorry," "I love you," "I want to do a better job of living out the values that I say I embrace," or to make midcourse corrections in your family's life today and the legacy you will leave tomorrow. It's a cliché, but it's true: Today is the first day of the rest of your life as a person and as a parent or grandparent. No matter where you find yourself, understand that our development as human beings is never a done deal. Endless possibilities and untapped potential wait to be revealed in all of us. It's not about how much we know but about how willing we are to learn, not where we stand but in which direction we are moving, not what doubts we harbor but to what truth such doubts eventually lead, not how we may appear in the eyes of other people but how much truth we are seeking in the quietness of our hearts.

Remember this: Whatever we as parents teach our children, consciously or unconsciously, each of them personally must come to terms with what he or she believes. We cannot force our views, values, or faith on them. We cannot control their choices. We can, though, give them a foundation—through our words and actions, the way we communicate, and the way we live our lives—from which they can start looking for answers.

Character is formed, not by laws, commands, and decrees, but by quiet influence, unconscious suggestion and personal guidance.
—Marion L. Burton

Maybe you're thinking right now that you feel good about what you've taught your kids. You've done your best to live out what you say you believe, and now, as they leave the nest, they're ready to make their own choices. You've given them the groundwork for creating a satisfying and successful life, but it's up to them to do so.

Or maybe you're thinking that you've blown it—maybe big-time in some areas—by not setting the kind of example you realize you should have or taking a stand on some issues that were clearly wrong, by overreacting or withdrawing affection when a child let you down, by not stopping to figure out for yourself how you feel about different issues you want your children to understand. Even now you are not sure where to start. But you do know that you want to do well by your children and their children. You want to provide them with every tool for living a successful life that you can.

It's never too late to be what you could have been.

—George Eliot (Mary Ann Evans)

IF YOU WANT THINGS TO CHANGE, THINGS HAVE TO CHANGE

When our first two boys were very young, I made a painful decision (at least it seemed so at the time) to become a morning person. My tendency to stay up and watch *The Tonight Show* was wreaking havoc on my family. I would set my alarm with good intentions to get up early, get my mind focused and my spirit centered so that I could greet my family and meet the day's duties with a peaceful, positive disposition.

It wasn't happening.

Readjusting is a painful process, but most of us need it at one time or another.

—Arthur Christopher Benson

Morning after morning I would push the snooze button on my alarm who knows how many times until I finally coerced myself out of the bed so that the kids wouldn't be late to preschool—again.

I realized that if I wanted things to change, I had to change. I bought an obnoxiously loud alarm clock and put it in the bathroom. This way I would have to get out of bed to turn it off. Unpleasant, but it worked. This small relatively small change made a big change in me personally as well as in my family.

As you read this chapter, here are couple of questions for you: Is an alarm going off in your life, and are you continuing to hit the snooze button? Maybe you feel that the issues you're facing are just too big to tackle. Maybe the changes look too complicated to make and the challenges seem too great to tackle. And besides, you're tired. You thought parenting was for young people. You've done your part, and you want to roll over and go back to sleep. Maybe the next time the alarm goes off, everything will have worked out and the problems will have disappeared.

Everyone thinks of changing humanity and nobody thinks of changing himself.

—Leo Tolstoy

It might happen that way in Lake Wobegon, but it doesn't in real life. Family issues and relationship problems just don't just go away. At some point we all have to wake up and realize that if things are going to change, we have to change. Simply put, we have to learn how to be the parents of adult children. We have to discover new ways to communicate and show our love; we have to define (or redefine) our goals and boundaries. Some of the rules we learned when we were parenting young children are the same—such as the fact that children need unconditional love to thrive—but many of the rules are different. We must keep learning and be willing to make some changes to have a loving, fulfilling relationship with our adult children.

In this book you've read a lot of ideas for possible changes. Because we are different—in personality, family makeup, where we live, where we work, our expectations—each of us will adapt and apply the ideas in different ways. But no matter who we are, every change we are willing to make for the good of our family is worthwhile.

SOME IDEAS TO GROW ON

The following thoughts and ideas are meant to spur your thinking about how you can pass down a legacy of strong values and strong character to your adult children as well as your grandchildren. Choose the ones that fit your family and adapt them in ways that seem natural to you. It's never too late to start—or to add to an already firm foundation.

We have only this moment, sparkling like a star in our hand . . . and melting like a snowflake. Let us use it before it is too late.
—Marie Beynon Ray

- Remember: What we leave in our children is far more important than what we leave *to* them.

- Set aside some time, either with your spouse or alone, to make a list of the values you want to pass on to your children and grandchildren. Here are some you might consider. Beside each characteristic that is important to you, jot down ways you are (or want to be) affirmative, attractive, and authentic in your communication of it.

Honesty _____

_____

Kindness _____

_____

Love _____

_____

Faith _____

_____

Patience _____

_____

Self-discipline _____

_____

Commitment to community service _____

_____

Loyalty _____

_____

Leadership _____

_____

Enthusiasm _____

_____

Love of learning _____

_____

Strong work ethic _____

_____

Courage _____

_____

Love of God _____

_____

Allegiance to country _____

_____

Patience _____

_____

Care for others _____

_____

Helpfulness _____

_____

Compassion _____

_____

Tolerance _____

_____

Respect _____

_____

- If you are the only parent committed to creating a positive legacy, gain strength from Helen Keller's words: "I am only one, but still I am one. I cannot do everything, but still I can do something; I will not refuse to do the something I can do." Don't give up; you don't know what good your efforts may do.

- Seek out a wise older mother or father to be your mentor during this passage in life. Although I am a mentor to women younger than myself, I still have many mentors who are older than I. We never grow too old or wise to benefit from those who are ahead of us in life.

- Start a collection of good books that teach strong character qualities and values to your grandchildren.

We have enjoyed *The Book of Virtues* by William Bennett. Ask a librarian or bookstore for other suggestions.

When a man dies, if he can pass enthusiasm along to his children, he has left them an estate of incalculable value.
—Thomas Edison

• When your children leave for college, remind them that they must stand for something or they'll fall for anything. Talk specifically about what they're willing to stand for.

• Did you get caught up in Woodstock, free love, drugs, and irresponsible living when you were a young adult? Talk with your older children about your hopes for them regarding living by strong values and how their experiences might differ from what you experienced when you were their age. Be honest about your own feelings without dragging out too much "dirty laundry."

What a father says to his children is not heard by the world, but it will be heard by posterity.
—Jean Paul Richter

• Remember Benjamin Franklin's advice: "One today is worth two tomorrows; never leave that till tomorrow which you can do today." Don't wait to begin a legacy of love and wise living for your children and grandchildren.

- Dr. Howard Hendricks once said, "First I make my decisions, then my decisions make me." The decisions we make daily form us into what we will be tomorrow. Small decisions can have a big result—for good or for bad. Talk about the implications of this adage around the dinner table sometime when you're all together.

Our souls are hungry for meaning, for the sense that we have figured out how to live so that our lives matter, so that the world will be at least a little bit different for our having passed through it.

—Harold Kushner

- Ask your children and grandchildren what they think is the meaning of this old adage: "You're not necessarily on the right track just because it's a well-beaten path."
- Take a look at yourself from your family's perspective. Do they look up to you as the type of person they want to be some day? Is anything in your life causing them to lack respect for you?

Evaluate your own personal spiritual journey. What legacy will you leave with your children? I encourage you to take time to ask hard questions and search for answers. Ask yourself honestly if what you believe adequately covers the serious issues of life. Does your faith give your life meaning, purpose, and peace? Does your faith support you in every phase of living: youth, young adulthood, middle age, old age, marriage crises, financial crises, children's crises, energy crises, cultural crises, and moral crises? Does it offer a healthy way to deal with guilt and forgiveness? Does it answer the question of evil and still give you hope? Does it provide a way for you to look realistically at the problems of life without despair? In my life, I have discovered the answers to these questions and guidance for becoming a good parent and grandparent in the Bible. I encourage you to search and come to terms with these questions in your own way—for your own sake as well as your children's.

All I have seen teaches me to trust the Creator for all I have not seen.

—Ralph Waldo Emerson

The family is the forming ground for the mortals in our midst. We initiate the moral standard bearing, the spiritual hunger, the legacy of love we hope our children will choose to emulate. What we do, say, and think teaches our family members "who they are and how to be that way"—in far-reaching ways. If you haven't already done so, begin today to build a worthy, lasting, and rich heritage for your children and your children's children. This investment can't help but make your home and the world a better place—and that is what family is all about.

10

The Portable Mom:
The Mother of All Resources

Learning makes a man fit company for himself.

—Thomas Fuller

*A*lthough it's enormously important for a young adult to leave home with a good head on his shoulders in regard to who he is, what he believes, and how he's going to interact with those around him, it really helps if he knows how to iron a shirt and pay the bills.

When our kids leave home, they will experience a realm that is quite possibly entirely new to many of them: taking care of all of their "stuff" and learning the ins and outs of managing a home, whether it's an apartment, a dorm room, or their few square feet of a barracks. Their new responsibilities will include things they may have taken for granted, such as cleaning and ironing clothing, protecting possessions, paying bills and managing cash flow, transporting themselves to and from classes and/or work, maintaining a clean home, and selecting and paying for health and life insurance.

Many years ago, when I moved away from home to attend college 400 miles away, I had never washed a load of laundry or ironed a piece of clothing in my life. On my first attempt at doing laundry, I loaded my clothes and the washing powder in the dryer. I couldn't for the life of me figure out how to turn the water on. There are many more stories I could tell about my lack of preparation to live away from home, but suffice it to say that over the years, as I taught myself the necessary domestic survival skills, I became a great advocate of parental involvement in this area.

To live effectively is to live with adequate information.
—Norbert Wiener

Actually, as parents we are always coaching our kids toward independence and responsible behavior. We're mothers for a lifetime. And even though our teaching may be subtle, we're still encouraging our kids—be they five or thirty-five—to move toward their full potential. Remember that even though now you're on the sidelines, you're still cheering them on and supporting them along the way.

In this chapter you'll find practical ideas for helping your offspring hit the field running. These are ways to teach older children life skills they need to know not only to survive, but to thrive in the real world.

YOUR YOUNG ADULT'S NEW WORLD

When I was a young mother, struggling to balance household, family, and personal issues, I realized something pivotal: the way businesses handle multiple tasks, through managing by department, could also work for a harried homemaker. I made a list of all the items I was responsible for and saw that they fell into seven departments: time, food, home and property, finances, special events, family and friends, and self-management.

Seeing my life and home through the eyes of a manager made the monumental task of juggling schedules, doing laundry, paying bills, and the rest of life's responsibilities infinitely more doable. This method of managing life worked so well for me and my family, I started writing and presenting seminars on the topic in the hope of helping others have the same success. Countless people have told me how it's made an enormous difference in their lives as well.

Managing by departments is something every person must do, whether she's married, single, a young adult or older adult, a parent or childless. Therefore, if we want to help our children get the best possible start into adulthood, we need to familiarize them with these departments and give them some pointers on organizing and running these areas in their own lives. For the young adult, responsibilities break down this way:

Time: Getting to classes and/or work and appointments on time

Food: Eating economically and nutritionally

Home and Property: Maintaining a reasonably clean and organized apartment/dorm/house and belongings

Finances: Managing budgets, bills, saving, investing

Special Events: Handling any responsibility outside the routine—holidays, birthday parties, vacations, special travel plans

Family and Friends: Building relationships with loved ones; nurturing friendships

Self: Nurturing oneself emotionally, spiritually, mentally, and physically

You'll give your young adult a leg up on life by sitting down sometime together and talking about each of these departments. Ask which departments your child feels confident about and which ones seem a bit foreign or fearful. Discuss the responsibilities he will be facing in each, and decide how he'll learn what he needs to know before he leaves.

For example, let's say your son is moving to another city to take a job and go to school at night to become certified in a certain trade. Here's what he may need to do in each department.

> *Time:* He's going to have to get himself out of bed in the morning, figure out how long his commute to work will be so he can arrive on time, budget time after work to study and go to class, and find some space during the week to work out at a gym. (You make a note to buy him a new alarm clock.)

> *Food:* He'll have to stock the kitchen in his apartment with basic pots, pans, and utensils, find out where the least expensive grocery store is, and try his hand at cooking. (You make a note to copy some simple recipes for him and clean out your pots and pans. You know there are some duplicates you don't need.)

> *Home and Property:* He'll have to do his laundry, find a dry cleaners, buy a vacuum, stock up on cleaning supplies.

> *Special Events:* He'll have to keep track of friends' and relatives' birthdays and special events, and decide how he'll handle them. (Suggest that he keep an assortment of greeting cards on hand; that he learn how to find supersaver fares on the Internet for when he wants or needs to travel.)

Family and Friends: He'll need to decide how he's going to stay in touch with loved ones on the home front—call or e-mail weekly? (Make a copy of all phone numbers and addresses—including e-mail—he will need; call your friends who live in the city where he's moving for information about the best places to shop, eat, get car repairs, and so on.)

Self: He'll have to find a gym and a church, and sign up at the local college for night courses.

COLLEGE: HELPING YOUR CHILD MAKE A SMOOTH TRANSITION

Here it is: the first almost-adult choice your teenager has to make, and it's a big one. Be sure to help all you can without forcing your choice on your son or daughter. The search should begin at least eighteen months in advance, and it shouldn't be influenced by your own fond memories of the old alma mater. Here are four things you should do:

1. Working together with your teen, research potential choices. Talk honestly about tuition and other expenses. Encourage your teen to share goals, concerns, and expectations.

2. Visit as many schools as you can. Check to see whether a college will be in session, and plan a meeting with someone from the admissions office. If the whole family can't attend, alternate visits with your spouse.

3. During senior year your teen will need to begin narrowing his or her choices. Help him or her create a compare-and-contrast sheet to see how different schools measure up. Rate each school in the follow-

ing categories from one to five, with five being the highest score:

- Annual tuition

- Living costs

- Availability of financial aid

- Availability of proposed major

- Other academic strengths

- Other benefits (good music department, strong sports teams, etc.)

- Distance from home

- Overall rank

4. Be prepared to fill out parts of college applications and financial aid applications and keep your tax records handy.

In the final analysis it is not what you do for your children but what you have taught them to do for themselves that will make them successful human beings.

—Ann Landers

---

5. Research scholarships. There are a wide variety of scholarships available, but you must apply to be considered. Check out www.fastweb.com for more information.

Departure Day Countdown

1. You and your spouse should each spend some private time with your teenager.

2. If your teen wants a going-away party, help put it together.

3. Shop together for necessities. Don't buy too many clothes; leave some money in the teen's budget so that he or she can purchase the "in" items at school.

4. Two weeks before departure, start packing. If your child will be traveling by airplane, ship boxes a week ahead; if you're traveling with him or her, purchase some items at your destination.

5. Plan a special family dinner for the college-bound teen. Consider putting together a *This Is Your Life* video program or displaying photos of the honoree's childhood in the kitchen or family room. Involve your other children in these opportunities to toast, or roast, their sibling.

6. Even if you plan to keep your teen's room as it is, with your teen's input, go through his or her files and bookcases, putting away school mementos. Sort clothing into piles to be packed, to be left at home, and to be given away.

7. Provide your teen with a credit card, carefully explaining what purchases are okay to use it on (see "Tips for Teaching Your Kids to Use Credit Cards Wisely" on page 237).

8. Create a family album. Slip it into the teen's luggage or present it when you arrive at the school. When she's homesick, flipping through the photographs will remind her how much she is loved.

9. Make plans to keep in touch by phone; a cell-phone with no-charge long distance, a prepaid phone card,

or a home 800 number is a good investment.
Or you could agree to communicate regularly by
e-mail if your child prefers that.

10. Remind your departing teen of the risky behavior
that happens on college campuses. Ask him or her
to consider personal values and boundaries when
faced with difficult choices.

LEARNING TO MANAGE MONEY

Not too long ago I ran into an old friend who had just attended
the college graduation of her youngest child. "Not only did she
graduate, she even has a job!" my friend exuded. "I'm not sure
what we're going to do with all the extra money since we're not
supporting our kids anymore." Nice problem, huh?

Few would argue that raising children is expensive. Very
expensive. But it's a priceless privilege for which most parents
would sacrifice their all. Yet there comes a time when Daddy's
money, or Mom's, as the case may be, needs to dry up and
the child become self-supporting. Unless you've prepared your
child for the responsibilities of financial independence, he
could be in store for a lot of pain and heartache.

---

*All the money in the world is no use to a man or his
country if he spends it as fast as he makes it. All he has
left is his bills and the reputation for being a fool.*
                                        —Rudyard Kipling

In Chapter 1 we looked at how our kids have been
brought up in a culture characterized by consumption. Unless
our kids have made some decisions about their priorities, it
will be easy for them to lose perspective about what's really

important. They'll end up making impulsive decisions and spending money they shouldn't spend. Or if they've reached the limit on their credit cards and can't spend any more money, unless they've decided what they value in life, they can easily feel insecure, discontent, and unable to enjoy the blessings of life they do have.

One of the most important life skills you can pass on to your children is how to handle money. Their ability to budget, make good buying decisions, and keep track of income and outgo will affect everything else they do. So do your kids a favor. Get them headed in the right financial direction by following these three steps:

1. *Help them form a financial philosophy.* Set a time to sit down together and talk about finances and the future. A good place to start is by having your adult child answer these questions. Suggestions you might make are in parentheses.

   - What does it mean to be productive? (We shouldn't expect to receive something for nothing. The accumulation of money requires work.)

   - What does it mean to be honest? (In addition to taking money outright, it's important to realize that we can steal nonmaterial things, such as time from an employer, credit for something someone else accomplished, someone's talent or services you use but don't pay for.)

   - What does it mean to be generous? (Sharing your resources and time with others is a good and personally satisfying thing to do. What ways do people get involved with religious organizations, local charities, and causes they want to support?)

- What does it mean to be secure in who you are? (Kids have grown up in a society that tells them they are valuable if they wear the right brand of jeans and use the right toothpaste. It's important that you understand that you are not what you own, wear, or drive. Each of us is valuable as a unique human being.)

- What do we deserve? (None of us always gets what he deserves. But most of the time, we will have more than we need. We need to count our many blessings and nurture contentment with what we have.)

2. *Help them establish financial priorities.* Once your young adult has his philosophy pretty well nailed down, he needs to set his priorities. Unless he makes some decisions about what he needs to spend money on, he will find it easy to spend it merely on things he wants. The result? Frustration, disappointment, and confusion. He can avoid this by considering:

- The five things he values most about his life today.

- The five things he wants that money can buy.

- The five things he wants that money can't buy.

- How much is enough? Have him complete these sentences: *I'll feel okay about money when I have $_____ in the bank. I'll be content when I have $_____ .*

- What causes he would like to support financially. How much would he like to give?

- Where he would like to be financially in twelve months—in five years—in twenty years.

- How he feels about going into debt—about getting out of debt.

- How he would finish this sentence: *If I suddenly found myself in a financial crisis, I could do without* _____ .

3. *Help them develop a financial strategy.* Once you've helped your child decide his philosophy and his priorities, you can give him a strategy to make those things happen. Before he leaves home, be sure he has his financial ducks in a row. He should have: a budget, a savings plan, an organized way to keep important records, a strategy for reducing debt if he has it, and the ability to file tax returns. In addition he should have insurance and know what it costs and what it covers, and he should be in the process of establishing good credit.

TIPS FOR TEACHING YOUR KIDS TO USE CREDIT CARDS WISELY

- Consider getting department store cards or gas company credit cards. These are usually smart choices for those beginning a credit history, as this type of card usually has low limits and can be paid in full each month.

- Always pay the bills on time or early.

- Consider an affinity card that provides miles or redeemable points.

- Keep your debt below 75 percent of the total available credit line.

- Always pay at least the minimum amount.

- If you can't afford the purchase, don't use the credit card—ever.

- Review statements carefully for fraudulent charges.

- Keep your personal identification number private.

- Review your credit reports annually.

MORE LIFE-SKILL BASICS

For your first-time-ever independent child, here are some tips that will make the daily grind much smoother.

Laundry

Doing laundry, according to the young adults in my family, ranks right up there with cleaning the oven. When one of my sons left home, he went so far as to buy 30 pairs of underwear, so he'd only have to do laundry once a month. Whether your child avoids doing laundry at all costs or likes to keep dirty clothes under control, it's important that he know his way around a laundry room.

When I went away to college, I felt very unprepared. My mother had a housekeeper who had always handled the laundry—I didn't know you couldn't wash red clothes with white. Also, I had never had experience paying bills, and when I got my first ones, I paid the utilities late—oops. Parents should teach their kids these kinds of things before they leave home.

—Stephanie, age 22

Here are some tips to pass on to your child:

1. Wash and dry with care. Separate whites that can take chlorine bleach (sheets, towels, socks) from delicate whites (lingerie, permanent press) that need nonchlorine bleach. Separate noncolorfast colors (jeans, dark towels) from the rest of the laundry. Separate slightly dirty articles from heavily soiled ones. Separate lint givers (chenille, towels, throw rugs) from lint receivers (corduroy, permanent press, socks).

2. Empty all pockets before washing clothes. Turn knits wrong side out to avoid snags and pilling. Zip zippers and button buttons to keep them from catching on things.

3. Use the amount of detergent recommended by the manufacturer. Dissolve powdered or liquid detergent and additives before adding clothes to the washing machine.

4. For minimum wrinkles, use fabric softener sheets, and load the dryer only one-third to one-half full. Cut down on ironing time by drying clothes loosely and taking them out of the dryer immediately after the cycle is done. Air-dry cotton clothes on plastic hangers, smoothing them with your hand.

5. Clean the lint filter after each load. Built-up lint can start a fire. And never put items in the dryer that have been in contact with flammables, such as gasoline, paint, or machine oil. The fumes could ignite.

6. Be careful with bleach. Only use it on white and colorfast washables; always read fabric and bleach labels. Never apply undiluted bleach directly to fabrics. If you are machine washing, add chlorine bleach manually or by the bleach dispenser, if your machine has one, after the wash cycle has begun. If you are hand washing, add it to the wash or the rinse water or both. Never use bleach and ammonia in the same wash. The combination can create hazardous fumes.

7. If a garment says "dry-clean only," take it to the cleaners. Test any garment labeled "dry-clean" for colorfastness before hand washing. Put the edge of an inner seam or hem on a paper towel and then saturate a cotton swab with cool water and press it down firmly on the fabric. If no color bleeds onto the paper towel, you don't need to have the garment dry-cleaned.

8. Do all your ironing at once rather than making frequent trips to get the board out and to heat up the iron. Ironing doesn't have to be a long, tedious job. It's a great task to accomplish while you're watching television.

9. Iron along the grain of the fabric. Circular or diagonal strokes can stretch fabric. Never iron silks on the right side. Avoid shine on wools and dark colors by

ironing on the wrong side or using a pressing cloth or ironing shield. If you spot a stain, don't iron the garment. Heat will make the stain permanent.

10. Use steam to your advantage: Hang a wrinkled skirt or shirt in the bathroom while you shower. The wrinkles may disappear, or at least the fabric will be ready for swift ironing.

QUICK TIP

Tell your child that if her laundry really piles up or if she's just come home from a trip with a lot of dirty clothes, she should go to a Laundromat and get it all done at once. If she's got four loads to do, she can fill up four washers and dryers, saving many hours.

SETTING UP HOUSE

Many kids never live in a dorm; an apartment, house, or rented room is their first home away from home. Therefore, they often need guidance on how to set up house for easy and functional living. Even an older child may not be aware of all the necessary ingredients for a well-stocked home. But no one wants to try to cope with an upset stomach in the middle of the night, slice cheese with a butter knife, or swab a major spill with bathroom tissue. To make sure your child is set for everyday as well as emergency situations, use the following checklist:

For the bathroom

Acetaminophen for pain and fevers

Adhesive tape (for use with gauze)

Air freshener

Antacids

Antibiotic ointment for cuts, scrapes, and burns

Antidiarrhea medication

Antihistamine for colds, allergies, and itching

Aspirin (only if your son or daughter is over twenty; its use has been associated with Reye's syndrome)

Bandages in a variety of sizes

Bar soap

Bath mat

Blow-dryer/curling iron

Burn medication

Cleaners for the shower, sink, toilet bowl, and floor

Cotton balls and swabs for applying medication

Decongestants/cough syrups (suppressant and expectorant)

Elastic bandage (Ace, for example)

Eyedrops (keep a large bottle to flush chemicals or foreign matter from eyes)

First-aid manual

Glass cleaner

Heating pad or hot water bottle

Hydrocortisone cream for rashes and other skin irritations

Hydrogen peroxide to clean wounds and disinfect minor cuts

Ice pack

Ibuprofen for muscle aches and swelling

Lip balm

Lotion for dry skin

Nail clippers

Plunger

Razors

Rubbing alcohol for disinfecting

Scissors

Shampoo/conditioner

Shower curtain

Sponges

Sterile gauze pads (four- by four-inch and two- by two-inch sizes) and rolls of gauze for wrapping

Sunscreen

Thermometer

Throat drops

Toilet brush

Toilet tissue

Toothpaste/brush/floss

Tweezers

For the Kitchen

Baking pans (A nine- by nine-inch square and a nine-by thirteen-inch oblong will give you a good start on baking anything from cornbread to chicken to brownies.

Consider the nonstick option if you go with metal. If you prefer glass, buy the oven-to-freezer-to-microwave type for maximum versatility. Consider a small broiling pan.)

Butter dish

Cake pans/storer

Can opener (A hand-held opener with a comfortable grip will do nicely. If you go electric, have a backup in case the power goes out and you need to make tuna sandwiches for dinner.)

Coffeemaker and filters

Colander (Metal or plastic is fine.)

Cookie jar

Cookie sheets (Buy heavy-gauge, nonstick cookie sheets. They'll last longer, be easier to clean, and burn fewer cookies than will their flimsy counterparts.)

Cooking-for-one cookbook

Cutting board (Buy the washable plastic kind that can be cleaned at the sink or put in the dishwasher.)

Dish drainer

Dishrags

Dish towels

Dishes (Don't forget mugs and serving dishes.)

Dishwashing detergent

Dry and liquid measuring cups

Foil, plastic wrap, and wax paper

Garbage bags (You'll need thirteen-gallon ones for the kitchen garbage can and bigger ones for outdoor barrels.)

Grater

Ice cube trays

Knives (Buy good ones: at least one paring knife, a serrated knife, and a chopping knife.)

Measuring cups

Measuring spoons (Get a set of metal spoons linked together; they are sturdy and can go in the dishwasher.)

Mixer (Look for a small hand-held one.)

Mixing bowls (Look for a nesting set of several bowls.)

Oven cleaner

Paper towels

Pastry blender

Pie plate

Pizza pan (Get nonstick.)

Place mats

Plastic containers for leftovers

Potato masher

Pot holders (Get a couple of flat ones and an oven mitt.)

Rolling pin

Rubber gloves

Salt and pepper shakers

Saucepans (Get large (holds three to four quarts), medium (two quarts), and small (one quart).)

Scrubbers for pots and pans

Self-sealing plastic bags

Skillets (Get an eight-inch nonstick for frying up a couple of eggs and a twelve- to fourteen-inch pan for stir-frying and sautéing. When you're skillet shopping, look for sturdy pans that will distribute heat well and resist warping.)

Small food chopper

Spoon rest

Tea kettle (Choose one that whistles and won't rust inside.)

Timer

Toaster or toaster oven

Utensils (Get wooden spoons, soup ladle, salad tongs, pasta grabbers, pancake turner, rubber spatula, wire whisk, and barbecue utensils.)

Vegetable peeler

For the Emergency Drawer

Battery-operated radio/alarm clock

Candles

Fire extinguisher

Flashlight

Fresh batteries

Lantern

Matches

Phone number for the utility company so that your child can report power outages

Phone number for the building manager for repairs

HOUSEKEEPING

For many young adults, housekeeping chores were something they did only if asked when they lived at home. Now they have to pick up and clean up after themselves. With all the other new responsibilities they're facing, you'll do them a favor by passing on some tips and shortcuts to make housekeeping easier.

Kitchen

- The first step in cooking or baking should always be to fill the sink with warm, soapy water. Toss bowls and utensils in the water as you finish using them. Soak grimy pans in warm, soapy water while you eat. After the meal, cleanup will much easier.

- Before working with messy foods, cover the countertop or sink with waxed paper or a ripped-open brown grocery bag to catch the mess. When finished, wad up the paper and throw it away.

- Don't dirty unnecessary dishes. Marinate chicken or steaks in zip-lock plastic bags instead of bowls or pans.

- After using your blender, partially fill it with warm water, give it a squirt of dishwashing liquid, and run it for a few seconds. Rinse it out, then turn it over and allow it to dry on a towel.

- Clean out your refrigerator every week the night before trash pick-up.

- Line the crisper drawers in your refrigerator with paper towels so you don't have to clean the drawer—just toss the dirty paper towel and replace with a clean one every two weeks or so.

- Place a piece of waxed paper in the bottom of your microwave to catch spills.

- Keep a clean trash liner at the bottom of your kitchen garbage pail. When it's time to empty the bin, a fresh liner is readily available.

Bathroom

- The best time to clean the bathroom is right after taking a shower, when the steam has loosened the dirt.

- Clean your tub without scrubbing by fill it with hot water and adding 2 to 3 cups liquid bleach. Allow the solution sit for 20 minutes or so. Drain the tub and rinse clean.

- Keep a toilet brush in a caddy next to the toilet. Give it a frequent swish. Treat your toilet to an overnight soaking of white vinegar once a week. By morning, it will be disinfected. Just flush clean.

- Allow cleansers a chance to work. Instead of rushing to wipe up tile cleaner as soon as you apply it, give it a few minutes to do its thing.

- Wrap a terrycloth rag around a screwdriver to clean out shower door tracks. Spray generously with all-purpose cleaner and make several passes along the track.

- Before mopping the bathroom floor, vacuum around a dry tub, toilet and sink to remove lint and hair.

- To remove mold from bathroom tile, soak a cotton ball in bleach. Press it into the yucky area and allow it to sit for a few minutes.

- Every now and then toss your bathtub mat in the washer with two or three bath towels. Ditto your vinyl shower curtain liner.

Closets and Drawers

- Undress near your closet and either hang up, put away, or toss clothing into a laundry basket as you remove it. Resist the temptation to drape it on a piece of bedroom furniture.

- Keep a box for extra wire hangers in your bedroom closet. When it's full, return them to the dry cleaner. Have a laundry bag in your closet for clothes to go to the dry cleaners.

- Use a tie rack not only for neckties, but also for belts, scarves, leotards, lingerie, ribbons, and so on.

- Keep a small wastebasket in your closet for tags, cleaner bags, and pocket or purse debris.

- Use readymade organizers or different-size boxes in drawers to corral little things such as curlers, cosmetics, and ponytail holders, or bigger things like socks and underwear.

- Don't use drawers as an emergency hiding place for clutter when company comes. It's too easy to forget it's there. Instead put clutter in a laundry basket and stash it in a closet. It will be easy to distribute and put away later.

- Have only one junk drawer, but have one. But to keep it under control, when you have an extra five minutes, like when you're waiting for water to boil or popcorn to pop, declutter your junk drawer a bit at a time.

- Keep bathroom drawers neat with a plastic silverware tray.

SHOPPING FOR GROCERIES

For many young adults, keeping the refrigerator and pantry stocked is a new idea. Food always seemed to appear there magically when they lived at home. Now that they're on their own, they have to learn to be their own genie. If this is their first time down the aisles—at least the first time being in charge of all the grocery shopping—suggest that they go to the store when it's not crowded and when they're not rushed.

The following tips will make it easier.

Nine Quick Tips for Smart Shopping

1. Avoid frequent trips to the store. You'll save time and money. Create a grocery shopping routine. Try to go to the grocery store once each week. Avoid long lines by shopping when others don't. Don't shop when you're hungry or tired. It's harder to make wise economical decisions at those times.

2. Keep an ongoing grocery list in a central location. When you open the last bottle or package of an item, add it to your list.

3. For healthier shopping, spend more time around the perimeter of the store, where there is fresh produce, bread, fish, meat, and dairy products. With the exception of cereals, grains, pastas, herbs, and some frozen foods, the inner aisles contain mostly processed or junk foods.

4. Don't assume that the larger size is cheaper. Check out unit prices. (A unit price is the cost for a small unit of measure, such as an ounce.) Be careful when companion foods are on display. The chips may be discounted, but the salsa could be premium-priced. Check top and bottom shelves; more expensive merchandise often is placed at eye level. And don't buy health and beauty items at grocery stores. Unless they are on sale, you usually can get them cheaper at a discount store or drugstore.

5. Check "sell by" and "use by" dates. Make sure you plan to use the food before expiration. Never buy a package that's dented, rusty, or torn.

6. Buy a few frozen entrees to keep on hand for busy days. Even pricey frozen meals are usually cheaper than takeout. Try no-frills and store brands. You may get the same quality the name brands offer. Compare the ingredients listed on labels to determine the similarity of products. Name brands and generics are sometimes identical.

7. Bag your own groceries so that you can put things together the way they go in your kitchen. If a clerk bags your groceries, make sure all the groceries get packed and every bag is placed in your cart.

8. Put grocery receipts in an envelope and save them for a month. You may need to return an unsatisfactory product.

9. Buy the freshest meat possible. Hamburger should be used within a day or two of purchase or frozen. Cook meat soon after buying it or rewrap it in freezer-quality plastic wrap before freezing. Meat displayed in the

meat department is wrapped in a special kind of plastic meant only for display; it breathes and helps keep meat a red color. Be aware that an expensive lean cut may be more economical than one that requires you to throw away excess bone, gristle, or fat.

BUYING THE FIRST HOUSE OR CONDO

The first major purchase is always a big deal. As a parent you can be incredibly helpful here. My friend Debbie has a stepson and a daughter-in-law with high-powered, time-consuming jobs. The lease was running out on their apartment, and they had to move out in a month. They wanted to buy a small house but had very little time to hunt for one. They called Debbie. She was honored: "I took a day off from work and made appointments with realtors. By the end of the day I had found a house I thought they would like. They came to see it after work, fell in love with it, and signed a contract for it that night. I could tell they sincerely appreciated my help, and I sincerely loved helping."

Your life experience in this area is invaluable, but not all kids will realize that. If your children ask for guidance, give it gladly; if they don't, let them make their best decision without you. It's their option since they're adults now.

Here are some steps you can suggest gently and respectfully, not forcefully:

1. *Examine the setting.* This is the single most important consideration, as the location of the house, apartment building, or duplex affects every aspect of your child's life. Look closely at where the housing sits in relation to streets and then check out the streets. Safety is the first priority.

2. *Scout the neighborhood.* Don't just look out the windows. Take a stroll for a few blocks in every direction. Do any local businesses threaten to force odors, noise, or traffic your child's way? Are yards messy or storage places for rusted cars? Are many homes for sale? Are grass and landscaping obviously cared for?

3. *Make a moonlight visit.* In whatever form of transportation your child will be using, travel to the proposed housing at night. How safe do you feel? Is the bus stop well lit? Who peoples the train station? Does your child have to travel far from his or her transportation drop-off to the house? Is traffic, a neighbor's dog, or a business causing a racket? Are creepy characters hanging around the parking area?

4. *Don't get shocked.* Ask about utility costs. Usually the electric company will tell you how much energy a previous tenant used during peak (winter and summer) months. If you are buying a home, examine the last year's utility bills.

5. *Turn every handle.* Test the water pressure as well all appliances and fixtures. Do the windows and doors open smoothly? Do the locks work? Do you see any signs of rain damage, moisture, or leaks? Do you notice any evidence of rodents or bugs?

6. *Survey the services.* Research what services are local: dry cleaner, post office, grocery store, bank, laundry. Are these places attractive?

7. *Examine the extras.* Explore what extras are available nearby: favorite eateries, someplace to take a walk, churches or synagogues, theaters.

8. *Meet the folks.* Introduce yourself to potential neighbors. Ask friendly ones how they like the building, neighborhood, or city. If you meet many crabby faces, beware.

9. *Be a legal eagle.* Ask the realtor to find out about property taxes, homeowner association rules, zoning ordinances, and assessments. If you're not satisfied with the answers, visit city hall and investigate for yourself.

THE STORY OF THE BIGGS AND THE LITTLES: A FASCINATING LESSON FOR CHILDREN AND PARENTS ALIKE

A friend of mine who teaches a class to soon to be-married couples at her church shared this story with me. The names have been changed.

Two young couples were shopping for their first home. Bill and Brenda Biggs found a home they liked for $125,000. It had three bedrooms, two baths, and a two-car garage. They had saved $10,000 for a down payment and could afford monthly mortgage payments of $1,000. They financed the other $115,000 for thirty years at 10 percent.

Larry and Lucy Little were also ready to buy their first home. They had $10,000 to put down and could afford $1,000 monthly mortgage payments, but they decided to investigate and study different approaches to house buying.

The Littles decided to buy a $70,000 cottage. It had two bedrooms, one bath, and no garage, but it had charming curb appeal and mature landscaping and was just right for their needs. They financed the remaining $60,000 for seven years at 10 percent.

At the end of seven years the Littles sold their cottage for exactly what they paid for it and bought a $125,000 home next door to the Biggses. It was a lovely three-bedroom, two-bath home with a two-car garage, very much like the Biggses' house. They put down their $70,000 and financed the rest for seven years at 10 percent. Their new payments were $913 a month.

Fourteen years later the Littles have paid $160,692 for their $125,000 home and now own the home free and clear. They decided to put the $913 a month into a pension plan.

The Biggses have now paid $165,000 for their $125,000 home and have sixteen more years to go at $1,000 a month.

After thirty years, Bill and Brenda make the final payment on their home. They have now paid $360,000 for their $125,000 home.

The Littles, after thirty years, own their home and have $353,000 in their pension fund.

MOVING

It's exciting, it's stressful, it's multifaceted, it's overwhelming—but it really is doable if you're organized. Use these ideas to make a move efficient and easy on everyone.

Before you move, don't forget to do the following:

- Arrange to transfer funds to a new bank and establish credit. Order checks with your new address.

- Arrange for insurance for your new home or apartment.

- Arrange with doctors, dentists, and eye doctors to have your records and prescriptions transferred or to take them with you. Make sure you have enough prescription medicine to get through a week in a new city.

- Notify the post office of your move and fill out change of address cards.

- Order address labels for your new home. You can use them to leave the new address with friends or businesses.

- Contact insurance agencies and other businesses you deal with regularly to let them know you're moving.

- Check on auto licensing and insurance requirements if you're moving to a new state.

A SHORT COURSE IN CRIME PREVENTION

No matter how safe the neighborhood appears to be, encourage your child to take the time to safeguard her or his home and its contents. Here's how:

1. Don't rent a house or apartment without dead-bolt locks.

2. Lock all doors and windows every night and whenever you leave your home. Most burglaries occur during working hours.

3. Make sure your door's hinges are on the inside. Pins in hinges on the outside are easy for a thief to remove with a screwdriver.

4. Avoid the most obvious hiding places for valuables: under mattresses, in nightstands, in jewelry boxes, in underwear drawers.

5. Make sure your doors have peepholes and use them before opening your home to a stranger.

6. If a stranger knocks and asks to speak with you, ask him to show ID before you open the door.

7. Don't hide a key in the usual places: under the doormat, on top of the door frame, in the mailbox, in a flower pot. Give a copy to a trusted neighbor or relative instead.

8. "Case" your own home for burglary: What unprotected entry points do you see? Better yet, call in the experts. Many police departments provide free security inspections for area residents.

9. Mark your possessions. Engrave valuable items with your Social Security or driver's license number or get a personal Operation ID number. Operation ID is a nationally sponsored program that makes personal property identifiable in the event of a burglary. The local police department should know where you can sign up for this service.

10. Get together with a few neighbors and create a Neighborhood Watch program. Don't overlook residents in apartments and condos. They need security too.

11. Keep trees and shrubs trimmed so that your yard is easily visible to neighbors and hard to hide in for thieves. Be on the lookout for easy access to the second floor from tall trees close to windows.

12. Plant bushes with thorns under your windows.

13. If someone asks to use your telephone, make the call for him or her rather than letting a stranger into your home.

Important! If you come home and notice that your house has been burglarized, leave immediately. Call the police on a cell phone or from a neighbor's house. Once the police arrive, you can go into the house and begin to take inventory of what is missing.

14. Make sure the doors and main-floor and basement windows are lit well.

15. Make sure the windows have locks.

16. Keep the garage door locked.

17. Don't leave major-appliance or electronic boxes on the curb after a purchase. These boxes alert thieves to your latest buys. Break down the boxes and tie them so that the wording doesn't show on the outside. If possible, dispose of them at a nearby dump.

18. Keep an eye on appliance repairpersons and cleaning people when they are in your home.

19. If you have sliding glass doors, make sure your landlord installs bolt locks on them.

20. Don't put your home address on luggage; use a business address.

21. Call the police if you notice any suspicious cars or persons in your neighborhood.

22. Lock up ladders and tools burglars could use to break into your home.

23. Display a "beware of dog" sign whether you have a dog or not.

24. Leave curtains open a little; a closed-up house signals it's empty.

25. Close curtains at night.

26. Don't put your address on your key chain.

IDENTITY THEFT ALERT!

Buy a paper shredder and shred mail that contains information about you. Criminals go through garbage looking for credit card and bank statements, pre-approved credit card applications, or anything that has a name or phone number.

Take the following precautions before leaving town:

27. Have the post office hold your mail when you're away; don't let a bulging mailbox signal your absence.

28. Ditto for the daily news. Stop delivery of newspapers when you're away or ask someone to pick them—as well as any packages that are delivered—up for you.

29. Before you leave on vacation, put your TV, lights, and stereo on timers. Set them to go on and off at different times, just as they would if you were home.

30. Leave a car in your driveway when you're away. Let a friend use the car or move it occasionally to make it look like you're home.

FIRE SAFETY

According to The National Safety Council, more than half a million residential fires occur annually in the United States. Most fatal home fires occur between 10 P.M. and 6 A.M. The major killer is smoke inhalation, not flames.

Smokey's right: Only you can prevent forest (or home) fires. Here's how:

- Ask your landlord to replace outlets and light switches that feel warm to the touch.

- Store flammable chemicals, including machines with gas tanks, in outbuildings or fireproof cabinets.

- Dispose of oil- or solvent-soaked rags safely to avoid spontaneous combustion. Never wad them while they are wet; hang or spread them to dry thoroughly, allowing the combustible elements to dissipate. Then dispose of them; consult the local waste-management authorities for requirements for the disposal of toxic materials. Don't dry or dispose of them near material that can ignite.

- Do not leave stovetop burners unattended. Always turn off burners when you leave the house, even for a short time. Avoid using hot settings for oil and foods that contain oil.

- Establish an escape route so that you can leave quickly in an emergency. Practice using it.

- Keep bedroom doors closed at night. This will slow the movement of dangerous smoke and gases while providing time to respond to fire-detector alarms.

- Have an A-B-C fire extinguisher on each level of your house, plus the kitchen and garage. Keep them fully charged and know how to use them.

- Wear short or close-fitting sleeves when cooking. Loose clothing can catch fire.

- Keep the oven door shut and turn off the heat to smother an oven or broiler fire.

- Always use safety screens in front of fireplaces.

- Make sure your apartment or house has at least one alarm on each level, using battery-operated or battery-backup alarms that detect both smoke and heat even when the power goes out. If you don't have smoke alarms, contact your landlord. Ideally, one should be in each bedroom and hallway.

COMMON EMERGENCIES AND HOW TO HANDLE THEM

It happens to everyone: the unexpected. Remind your grown child that she can't prevent sudden emergencies but good preparation and a little know-how can keep a bad situation from becoming worse. When Dad or Mom can't come to the rescue, here's what she can do:

Grease fire. Never throw water on a grease fire. If the fire is small, turn off the burner and smother the flames with a lid or a damp towel. Baking soda also will douse flames, so keep a box handy. Keep a fire extinguisher (chemical or foam, not water-based) stored in the kitchen where it can be grabbed easily, not in the cabinet space above a burning stove.

Electrical fire. Unplug the appliance and use a fire extinguisher (chemical/foam, not water-based) to douse the flames. Or smother the appliance in a heavy blanket or rug. Never throw water on a burning appliance.

Overflowing toilet. Turn the stop valve clockwise underneath the toilet to shut off the water. Bail out half the water with a cup and a bucket. Use a plunger to open a clogged toilet. (Put petroleum jelly on the lip of the plunger to help stabilize its position on the drain hole and then place the plunger securely over the bowl's drain hole and pump the plunger up and down.) If plunging doesn't work, call the landlord or apartment manager.

Gas leaks. If you smell a strong gas odor, extinguish all fires, cigarettes, and open flames and open as many windows as possible. Get everyone out of the house immediately. Call your apartment manager or the emergency service number of your utility company from a neighbor's house. Cut off the supply of gas to the house by turning off the valve beside the gas meter. If the odor is faint, check pilot lights to see if one has gone out. If one has, wait for the gas smell to diminish and relight the pilot. If you can't find the source of the odor, call for emergency service.

No electricity. Check to see if all the lights in your neighborhood are off. If only you are without power, turn the main switch at the top of your breaker box off and then back on. (The breaker box, sometimes called a service panel, is usually in a closet, the basement, or the utility room.) Shut off and unplug all appliances and electronics; they might draw a rush of electrical current when power is restored and could damage fuses and circuitry. Switch on appliances and lights one at a time.

Loss of heat. For gas heat, check to see if pilot light is burning; then relight it, following the manufacturer's directions. For electric heat, check for a blown fuse or tripped circuit breaker. Call the apartment manager or a repairperson if necessary. Shut exterior doors and close all curtains and shades except those which allow in direct sunlight.

Sink clog. Bale out water into a bucket. Boil a large pot of water and pour it down the drain. If this fails, position a plunger over the drain and push it down forcefully three times. Repeat if necessary. If you feel up to the task and if the blockage is in the U-bend pipe, place a bucket underneath and unscrew the U-bend. Carefully poke a piece of wire up the pipe until you free the obstruction. If this doesn't work, call a plumber.

BE PREPARED FOR DISASTER: FOUR THINGS YOUR CHILD SHOULD DO

Natural disasters—hurricanes, floods, wildfires, tornadoes, earthquakes—strike suddenly. Taking the necessary steps can make the difference between life and death. Make sure you're ready.

- Twice a year, designate the day you adjust the clocks for daylight savings time and then back to standard time as the occasion to change the batteries in smoke detectors and see that fire extinguishers and flashlights are in working order.

- Make an inventory of all your possessions and keep a copy in a safe place away from your home. Take several photos of valuable items.

- Make sure you know how to turn off the water, gas, and electricity at main switches.

- Keep the following emergency phone numbers handy so that you can call when you have a crisis:

  - Emergency services (fire, police, and ambulance)

  - The landlord or apartment manager

  - The nearest hospital

  - Physician, dentist, and pharmacist

  - Poison-control center

  - Emergency numbers for gas, electric, and water companies

  - Neighbors

  - Immediate family

  - Taxi

  - Veterinarian

Emergency Preparation Plan

Follow these steps:

- Identify the safest places in your house in case of a tornado or earthquake.

- Practice emergency evacuation drills.

- Learn first aid and cardiopulmonary resuscitation (CPR).

- Keep important records in a waterproof and fireproof container.

- Post emergency telephone numbers near telephones.

Disaster Supplies Kit

FEMA (the Federal Emergency Management Agency) and the American Red Cross suggest that each home have a disaster supplies kit. Store supplies in an easy-to-carry container such as a backpack or duffel bag. Include the following items:

- A portable, battery-powered radio or television and extra batteries

- A flashlight and extra batteries

- Matches in a waterproof container

- A first-aid kit and prescription medications

- Credit cards and cash

- Personal identification

- An extra set of car keys

- An extra pair of eyeglasses

- A signal flare

- A map of your area and the phone numbers of places you could go

- Blankets or a sleeping bag

INSURANCE

Teach your children to think of insurance as a protection plan against any problems: home, health, and car. It's important to take the time to understand how much and what types of insurance they need.

Homeowner's or Renter's Insurance

When he or she buys the first home, your young adult will be required to have homeowner's insurance. If your child rents a home or apartment, it's equally important. To determine the replacement value of what you own, insurance agents recommend creating a videotape inventory of your possessions—room by room—so that any claim for theft, fire, or flooding is backed up with visual documentation. Include all the items you own: furniture, electronics, jewelry, and clothing. Filming your possessions is also a good idea.

Health Insurance

As a parent, you know that health insurance is a necessary part of responsible adult living. One major illness or injury—and remind your child that such things are always unexpected—could lead to debt that sets your son or daughter back financially for years. Insurance is no less necessary than food, water, and clothing. Strongly urge your child to get some; if he balks, give him a reality check: Show him a few bills that list what you paid and what your insurance company paid.

If your child is lucky, her employer will offer health insurance for which your daughter has to pay only part of the premium each month. If your child is self-employed or works for a company that doesn't offer benefits, she will have to get her own insurance. Finding a broker is usually helpful; the broker will determine your child's needs and preferences and then examine the policies of a number of insurance companies. Together, your child and the broker can choose the best match and get the coverage started.

For a child who has to find his own insurance, here are some tips:

1. *Determine your needs.*

   • Do you have any preexisting medical conditions?

   • Is it important for you to use your already established doctors, or could you work with a new person from a preassigned list?

   • Are you willing to visit a primary-care physician before he or she refers you to a specialist?

   • How large a deductible and monthly premium can you afford?

   • Do you visit the doctor often for chronic conditions, such as asthma, allergies, and sports-related injuries?

   • Do you need dental and vision coverage?

   • Do you take a large number of prescription medicines?

2. *Compare plans and benefits.* See how much each company pays for

   • Pharmacy costs

   • Doctor visits

   • Specialist visits

   • Physical exams

   • Lab work

- Immunizations

- Hospital care and length of stay

- Inpatient surgery

- Outpatient surgery

- If needed, vision and dental care

3. *Cover your bases.*

- Examine a number of companies and plans. They vary widely.

- Ask all the questions you have to ask to understand the details of coverage.

- Be honest about preexisting conditions.

- Review your coverage annually to make sure it's meeting your needs.

- Consult insurance agents and agency and insurance industry Web sites and talk with your friends to see what types of packages and rates are available.

Auto Insurance

Another essential, auto insurance assures that you are able to pay for auto repairs or injuries you incur with your car. Help your young adult understand that there are several types:

1. *Collision:* If you hit another car or something else, this policy covers all repairs to your car regardless of who is at fault.

2. *Bodily injury liability:* This policy covers family members and friends you allow to drive your car in case they accidentally injure someone.

3. *Personal injury protection:* This policy covers your medical expenses if you or a family member gets injured in your car or someone else's.

4. *Comprehensive physical damage:* This policy covers the repairs needed because of fire, theft, and other mishaps.

5. *Property damage liability:* This policy takes care of claims and legal costs if your car harms someone's property. It does not cover repairs to your vehicle.

6. *Uninsured motorist:* If an uninsured driver hits or your car or your car is damaged in a hit-and-run accident by an unknown driver, this policy takes care of medical costs and repairs.

Make sure to do the following:

- Determine what kinds of car insurance your state requires.

- Check out discounts for good grades, taking a driver's training course, a clean record with no accidents, or car features such as antitheft devices, air bags, antilock brakes, and automatic seat belts.

- Get a minimum of three quotes and make sure the insurance companies providing the quotes are financially reputable. The Web sites for the National Association of Insurance Commissioners, Standard & Poor's, and Moody's Investor Services all provide this information.

- Make sure your selling agent or insurance broker is reputable. If you don't see an agent license number or if the agent can't provide one, contact your state's insurance bureau.

- Never pay cash for premiums and make the check payable to an insurance company, not an individual.

- Always get a copy of the policy you're considering in writing. Go over it carefully and make certain all the details are correct and agreeable to you.

- Clearly understand what a policy does not cover. For example, are rental car costs included? If they are not, consider purchasing supplemental insurance to cover this expense.

LIFE INSURANCE

Life insurance is important for young people as well as old. The fact is that everyone will need to be buried someday, and this insurance helps cover those costs so that your loved ones don't have to. It also can serve as an investment tool.

Determining How Much You Need

The standard rule is to purchase life insurance equal to between five and ten years of your annual salary, but individual circumstances vary. Suggest that your young adult ask herself the following questions to assess her needs:

- How much money do you spend a year on housing?

- What are your annual food and clothing costs?

- How old are your children? Younger children require care for more years.

- What primary and secondary school expenses are forthcoming?

- What amount of college tuition bills do you expect?

- Do you have other savings and investments to offset any of these expenses?

- What is an appropriate amount to set aside for any medical situations or emergencies?

Types of Life Insurance

There are two basic types of life insurance policies: term and permanent. Premiums for each of these two types can be either fixed or variable.

Term Insurance

Term life insurance lasts for a specific term or period and has no savings component. There are five kinds of term insurance:

- *Renewable term.* Permits you to renew at the end of each term without taking a medical examination. Premiums increase as you age.

- *Convertible term.* Allows a switch from term to permanent without a medical exam. The premiums are slightly higher than those for renewable term.

- *Level term.* Provides a fixed premium cost for a specific period of time. Premiums will increase significantly when the level term expires and a new policy is issued.

- *Decreasing term.* Over time the death benefit payout amount decreases, while the premium remains constant.

- *Increasing term.* The death benefit increases every year, along with the premiums.

Permanent Insurance

Permanent insurance usually is provided for the length of a person's life. The four kinds of permanent insurance are as follows:

- *Whole life*: The policy has a fixed rate and guarantees a cash value. A joint life policy is purchased by couples, and when one dies, the other receives the death benefit amount. Survivorship life covers a couple also but pays the death benefit only after both die.

- *Universal life*: Allows for changes in the death benefit and premium payments.

- *Variable life*: More of an investment option; the amount of any payout equals the performance of a preselected portfolio of investments.

- *Variable universal*: A combination of variable and universal.

Choosing between the Types of Insurance

Keep these facts in mind:

- Term is usually better for single young adults and those with young families because the rates are lower and the coverage dates are flexible.

- Term has no savings component. As you get older, the premiums increase, as does the probability of a medical exam before coverage is granted.

- Permanent offers a lifelong constant premium rate and should be considered a long-term investment tool.

- Permanent usually requires no medical examination past the initial one.

Buying the Policy

- Obtain at least three quotes before making a decision.

- Compare rates on-line, from insurance companies directly and from independent insurance salespeople.

- See if memberships in any clubs or professional groups entitle you to less expensive insurance.

- Determine if your selected insurer is financially sound by contacting a state or national rating agency.

It is wonderful to be young, but it is equally desirable to be mature and rich in experience.

—Bernard Baruch

YOU NEVER STOP BEING A MOTHER

At the beginning of this chapter, I told you how I started young adult life domestically challenged—to put it mildly. Many years later, I laugh with my delightful, ageless mother (she stopped having birthdays a few years ago) about how, in spite of it all, I have become quite an accomplished home and family manager. While Mom didn't teach me many household how-tos when I was young, she did something equally useful: she taught me lots of business and people skills from her retail clothing business. And when she retired, she started passing on tips about how to live life and run a home better. Even today she sends new recipes, the latest tips on how to get stains out, and continues to encourage me to take care of myself. She's still my mother.

It's never too late to start helping your child live a fuller. more productive life. And whatever you can pass along now has value. Know that because of your life experience, you are always a source of insight and instruction to your children, whatever their ages. And these ideas, shared with love and sensitivity, pave the way for your children's success in the world.

Parting Words

*I*t's both good and bad news: Parenting is never finished. The flighty highs, the crashing lows of raising responsible kids—they're all ours to keep for as long as we live. If this truth makes you feel tired, you're not alone; if it makes you feel elated, you're in good company, too. The bottom line is this: We've signed up for one of the most thrilling challenges and exciting adventures life has to offer. Your role—from delivery room to dorm room to dining room (once again furnished with high chairs and booster seats)—is a critically important one. Cut yourself, and your kids, plenty of slack and enjoy the process. Whether you're waving good-bye to your college-bound daughter or welcoming grandchildren, courtesy of your son, do your part to create healthy and happy relationships with your adult children. Family is for life, and it's one of the life's greatest blessings.

Warmest regards,
Kathy Peel

Index

About the Author

Kathy Peel is the founder and president of Family Manager Inc., a company dedicated to providing helpful resources to strengthen busy families and make the home a good place to be. She has served as Contributing Editor to *Family Circle* Magazine for ten years and writes frequently for other publications such as *American Profile*. She is a popular speaker, frequent guest on television and radio programs, and the author of numerous books, including *The Family Manager's Everyday Survival Guide* and *Be Your Best*.

Visit www.familymanager.com to learn more about Kathy Peel's appearances and speaking schedule. Please e-mail any comments or questions about this book to familymanager@familymanager.com.